900691

Roald Amundsen

A SAGA OF THE POLAR SEAS

By J. Alvin Kugelmass

KINGSTON HOUSE • CHICAGO

Roald Amundsen

A Saga of the Polar Seas

Books by J. Alvin Kugelmass

J. ROBERT OPPENHEIMER and THE ATOMIC STORY

LOUIS BRAILLE: Windows for the Blind

RALPH J. BUNCHE: Fighter for Peace

ROALD AMUNDSEN: A Saga of the Polar Seas

For ELIZABETH, JOEL *and* ELISE

and

GERTRUDE BLUMENTHAL, *Kindest and Wisest of Editors*

Contents

Roald Amundsen

A Saga of the Polar Seas

CHAPTER I

CHAPTER I

The Perilous Plateau

A famous mountain climber was once asked, "Why do you want to climb Mt. Everest?" His answer was simplicity itself. "Because it is there," he said.

Why do men brave the mountainous seas in small boats or on rafts? Why do they plumb the dark and mysterious depths of the oceans in fragile craft of their own designing? Why do they hazard death in charting great rivers in unexplored sections of great continents? Why do they trek across deserts and tundras and steppes seeking the far-beyond where no man has trodden before? Why do they pioneer in new planes testing their skill and strength against the sweeping currents of air and the illimitable ceiling above? The answers to these questions are many, for they may combine reckless courage with the love of adventure. But mostly the answer lodges in the same simple statement: the challenge is there and it must be met.

Man, indomitable man, since time immemorial has been confronting the challenge of his world and slowly and painstakingly besting it. Many men, in seeking to overcome the trackless seas, the towering mountains, and the frozen wastes, have lost their lives. Many have been forever lost and their bodies never found. But through the centuries what one man has vainly attempted and failed to achieve has been a touchstone to the next hero who followed in his path.

These men who have fought and failed are the legendary adventurers. The world pays them the homage, the very same tribute, accorded those who have won. But it is, of course, the triumphant adventurer who achieves the colorful glitter that always accompanies success.

This story is about a fabulous Norseman who adventured most of his life inside of the dim and far-off twilights of the North Pole and the South Pole. His name is Roald Amundsen, one of the very few giants of exploration on ice who won, in most cases, what he set out to do. And he did it at a time when only the dog sled and his own fierce will could avail him.

A glacier, a vast rearing colossus of ice; a gulf hemmed by ice; a frosty sea—these are the geographical monuments, all icy, named in his memory. He did not die a long time ago (and his death is classical, picturesque; perhaps the kind he would have wanted); yet wherever men of polar knowledge gather to talk, they speak of him as one might speak of a titan of the past. He charted and discovered a good section of the world which is only now becoming important—in terms of trade, peace, and war.

Roald Amundsen—the magnificent Norseman, as he is called—was born on July 16, 1872, on a tiny farm just a few miles south of Oslo, Norway. When he was an infant his family, of which he was the youngest child, moved to the city proper and he entered a primary school at the age of six. In common with all Norwegian children, just as soon as he could walk he was introduced to ice skates, skis, and snow-shoes. Snow and ice were a commonplace to him.

Living in a country whose northernmost regions jut into the Barents Sea hard by the Arctic Ocean, Roald's introduction to language naturally had to do with such words as *cold, ice, snow,* and *freezing.* When he began to read, his elementary texts treated of the exploits of the ancient Norsemen who had thought nothing of sailing far and wide in the regions of the icebergs. Always his young imagination was peopled with these hardy men of vast strength who put out into the great, frigid seas and the biting wind on tiny craft. Often he imagined himself at the prow of a Viking vessel, his eyebrows coated with ice, peering into the dark and gray wastes of the tumultuous seas.

When he was nine years old, he was entered in what is called a "gymnasium" in Europe. It is not the gymnasium as we know it here but, rather, a kind of junior high school or secondary school that prepares European children for college.

His father died when he was fourteen years old and his two older brothers left home to work at trades. He was left alone with his mother, who had one hope for her youngest. She wanted him to become a doctor. Accordingly she encouraged him to take courses which would best fit him for medical training. Meantime he became obsessed with books about great explorers and navigators. He read about Magellan, who went around the world; about Balboa, who discovered the Pacific Ocean; and, of course, about Christopher Columbus.

But these warm-seas navigators never seemed to hold the fascination for him that he found in tales about the icy-seas adventurers. Somehow he felt more akin to the men in furs who manned the vessels which foraged in the northerly regions than he did to those who were becalmed in equatorial waters of the world. These books inflamed him and he consciously began to harden himself to the rigors and the bite of cold winds. It was an early training for what came later and he tried to work at it daily.

His doting mother scolded him endlessly and often said that he was "touched" in the head. But she felt sure that with time the adolescent would settle down to a career in medicine. One of the things that infuriated her most was Roald's habit of sleeping in his dormer room with the windows wide open to the Arctic breezes that swept in furiously and coated his room with a patina of frost. "Shut your windows," she would shout, and the boy would pad across the icy floor in his bare feet, expose his naked chest to the vicious wind, and shut them. As soon as he was sure his mother was asleep, he would again open them.

At this time he came under the spell of the stories about the great British explorer Sir John Franklin, who had tried more than a dozen times to sail westward across the top of the world in a fruitless search for a Northwest Passage. Sir John was sure that there was a short route from the North Atlantic Ocean to the North Pacific Ocean if only some way could be found to skirt the vast icebergs and frozen fields. The Briton had been foiled time after time either because his ships became frozen in or because his men died from starvation or exposure.

Unknown to his mother, Roald began to gnaw on his leather boots to see whether he could subsist on the same rations that kept Sir John and his men alive for a space of three weeks when they were battling their way back to civilization. The boot leather was unpalatable, difficult to rend with the teeth, and he had a bad time trying to force shreds of it down his throat. His mother wondered about the boots and Roald pacified her by saying that he had scraped them on icy formations while skiing.

He also gnawed on bones which he stole from the kitchen garbage in imitation of Sir John's account of finding several in an abandoned Indian village into which they had stumbled during their heroic trek across ice floes and limitless snowy wastes. Sometimes he deliberately starved himself to see whether he could go without any food at all for days. He scooped snow into his mouth and allowed it to melt and trickle water down his throat. And he followed this regime for several years.

Because he could not withstand his mother's pleas he entered college at fifteen. It was understood that upon graduation he would allow himself to be enrolled in medical school. But this day seemed far off and in the meantime he continued his home training at every opportunity in order to harden himself for the life of the explorer. These boyish dreams seemed foolish simply because they were romantic. And yet the course of his fantastic life shows that he was dedicated to his dream—and, unlike most men, he realized his dream.

His reputation among the neighbors was none too good, for they, as well, thought he was "touched" in the head because he kept his windows open while they fastened theirs down as is the custom in cold countries. Too, they often saw him deliberately founder in snowdrifts and endure the penetrating cold of snow that entered his clothing. In those days there were few sports at Norwegian schools. Roald didn't particularly care for soccer, yet he joined the team and played it passionately in order to strengthen his muscles and inure his body.

He deliberately sought out blows and kicks from fellow players and flung himself down hard on the ground with the two-fold purpose of accustoming himself to pain and developing his will to endure pain. While this may sound ridiculous perhaps, a similar, if less rigorous training, is a matter of course for football players who want to make the team or for boxers in training.

At every oppourtunity he sought out the rigorous. During the months when the weather was fiercest, from November through April, he was rarely home on his days off from school. He went out, usually alone, to traverse the craggy mountains that ring Oslo. He preferred to be alone, for he wanted to test himself against the rugged terrain and the elements without having to explain to a school chum why he was doing so.

He used his ice pick to climb overhanging ice-laden cliffs and by sheer dint of will he would get to the top and fling himself down panting and exhausted. He clipped along at high speed on his skis, daring the naked pines in his way. He took very little food with him on his "picnics" and he made long journeys back home after dark had fallen and his mother was almost frantic with worry. He deliberately skimmed on his snowshoes across crusty surfaces until early twilight dropped down at four o'clock, so that he would have to retrace his steps in the dark knowing surely he would not return to safety until midnight. No remonstrances of his mother kept him from continuing this practice. However, in order not to worry her, he told her that he was studying at the library or with a class-mate.

His mother believed him and soon began to think that her best-beloved son was maturing and settling down. He did well at school, though his interest was slight. Somehow he found that his studies were easy for him and did not tax his energies. He proudly attributed this to the fact that he could now go with little sleep and could concentrate at will without getting tired.

At eighteen he was graduated from college with high honors and entered the University of Oslo to pursue his medical studies. His mother was delighted and from the small funds she had remaining she outfitted him with his first grown-up suit complete with high collar and a stock—a kind of ascot worn at the time. The boy-man was now more than six feet of lean, wiry ruggedness and showed, even at this early age, the erosion of wind and cold on his hatchetlike face. His impressive body formed a triangle from his wide shoulders down to his slender hips.

Two years later—after his mother, Anna, died—he was bereft of family and all alone. As he afterward related, though the death was a shock he felt shorn of all emotional ties. "With enormous relief, I soon left the university to throw myself wholeheartedly into the dream of my life." This was, of course, polar exploration.

In his mature years, when he spoke of his mother's death, he said he was glad that she was spared the shock of realizing he had no interest at all in doctoring the sick but was concerned only with Arctic exploration, a thing she surely would not have understood. How could she possibly have comprehended the drive of a boy taken up completely with a career so outlandish?

Soon after he left the university he was called up for compulsory army training. He was glad to go into military service, for he not only felt it was his duty as a citizen but realized that the exercises would still further prepare him for the arduous life he had charted for himself. From start to finish, his career was a blueprint for adventure and hazard and struggle.

Army medical directors were astonished by his physique. "Where did you ever get such muscles?" they asked. He was indeed a superb specimen. His leg and arm muscles were bold and knotty. His abdomen was lean and almost concave; his neck was a thick pillar and his spring was agile and light as a gazelle's. Only his eyes were below par. For years he had been told to wear eyeglasses but had never done so—chiefly, as he said, because he refused to recognize any defect in his body.

The examining doctor, however, completely forgot about the eyes in his astonishment at the magnificent frame. He called in other physicians and officers to look at Roald—a "regular Greek paladin," as the fascinated physician put it. Amid the confusion and flattering comments that followed, the regular eye test was overlooked. For the rest of his life Roald's near-sight remained troublesome, though his far-sight was excellent. This, for a man with the far horizon in view, was a perfect compensation.

He enjoyed the army, worked hard at his training, and was urged to make military service his career. But he had other ideas. At the time, compulsory military service in Norway just involved several weeks of concentrated training each year. Thus Roald had free periods to work at his own secret concept of how he was going to spend his life.

One day he decided to take the first step. It was a mad and foolhardy one, for it almost cost him his life. None of his later adventures, he declared, was as dangerous as the one he now undertook. But it was a test he had to make. He broke all rules in doing so and emerged a triumphant if badly frightened victor.

The project was incredible. West of the city of Oslo there is a range of almost vertical mountains. Atop of this, extending westerly almost to the city of Bergen on the Atlantic Ocean, a distance of more than one hundred and fifty miles, there is a plateau lying about six thousand feet above sea level.

Near the west coast of Norway and not far from Bergen, the great plain drops off sharply in an almost abrupt descent. During the milder months of the year the high plain is used by the Lapps for pasturing their herds of reindeer. The Lapps, a short, stocky, hardy group of the Mongoloid race, who know the plateau well, shun it during the frozen-in period.

These nomadic people drove their reindeer where it best suited them, and always left the plateau when winter fell. Here and there they had put up huts for shelter during the cold rainfalls of the autumn. Otherwise the plateau was deserted and unused by farmers.

On the easterly edge of the broad flatland, there was a single farm called Mogen; on the westerly edge, just before the almost vertical descent to the coast, there was a small farm called Garen. No one had ever attempted to cross from Mogen to Garen during the wintertime. Roald decided to do it. Exactly why he did so, he could never rightly tell—except that he felt it would be the test, the sinewy test before he went on to his dream.

He selected one companion. It was the dead of winter, during the Christmas holidays. He looked fondly at his boots and hoped he would have to chew on them. Mad? Yes. In later years he said that if he had known then what he had since learned he never would have tried the stunt. "It was only much later on that I discovered just how lucky I'd been. I doubt if I had a more harrowing time in my life."

His friend Leif Björnsen, about his age, never forgot the adventure and was ill for a long time afterward.

The pair made their way on skis across the treeless plain covered with a thick blanket of snow. As far as they could see across the white-upon-white flatness, there was nothing but a cloudy sky and a fine snowfall. They made tracks rapidly and soon came to Mogen. The farm was just a hut and the old man, his wife, and their two married sons and their wives had just closed themselves in for the winter.

The Mogen people were kind but chiding. "No, you cannot cross the plateau," they said. "Stay here and rest and then go back." They did not believe the two young men.

Early the next morning a great blizzard came up and the eight persons stayed in the small hut and slept and ate and exchanged small talk. This went on for more than a week. Then the snow no longer fell and Roald got out of a window to see what the crystal-clear, dazzling-white world was like, and sank into more than fourteen feet of drift. They pulled him out with a rope.

Roald and Leif adjusted their packs, said good-by to their kind hosts, and started off on snowshoes. The three men of Mogen followed them and begged them to think better of it. "You won't make it," they shouted. "Come back and go home." The two young men waved and sped on. "No one has ever done it," shouted the old man. "Not in the seventy years that I've lived here." Roald waved and soon the two were black specks in a great sea of white that steadily rose in a gradual elevation to a far-off point that could not be seen with the naked eye. The three men returned to the hut shaking their heads. "They are lost forever. The Lapps will find them in the spring."

CHAPTER II

Round Cape Horn
to Antarctica

The two sped on, ever rising to the lip where the plateau began. From a map he had found at the university library, Roald was sure they could shorten the route by almost half if they plunged ahead directly to the sea. With good luck, if the weather held, he estimated the trip at about two days.

The packs they carried were light. Just a few crackers, three bars of chocolate apiece, a spirit lamp, and sleeping bags made of reindeer hide with the fur turned inside. They also had a compass, ski sticks, and skis. Soon the snow packed down and they changed from snowshoes to skis. Thereafter the going was easier and speedier. They did not talk much but pressed on swiftly except for time out to consult the pocket compass. There were no landmarks at all, just the snow spread like a blanket on the vast circle of the horizon and the indistinct low hills on the fringe. The atmosphere was grayish and of the semitwilight variety that characterizes the period of the year when the sun merely glances over the top of the world.

Before evening they came on one of the herders' huts. The temperature was some forty degrees below freezing point and it was good to see the wooden shack. However, the door was nailed tight and they could see that the chimney was blocked up with twigs to keep the snow out. Leif climbed the side of rough boards and soon cleared away the twigs. But in the process he discarded his thick gloves and suffered a bad frostbite which almost cost him a thumb.

They broke into the house and soon had a roaring fire going. They ate a bar of chocolate, congratulated each other, rolled up in the sleeping bags and, after listening to the howling wind that screamed through the cracks, fell into an uneasy and drafty slumber. During the night another storm blew up, and in the morning they knew they couldn't go on.

For two days they lived in the hut rationing themselves on melted snow, small fires, and a bite of chocolate. Leif's finger looked bad and Roald, from his reading, knew enough to melt some fat out of his reindeer sleeping bag and apply a poultice. He wondered whether he really was made for this kind of hardship and the played with the idea of going back to medical school. This was different from what he had expected. In the books he had read, the hardship was glamorous and noble and self-sacrificing—attended by pain and discomfort, of course, but nothing like this hunger which gnawed at him and this cold which buffeted him with every blast that came through the chinks in the hut. When he looked outside he was frightened by the driving snow and the tremendous drifts. He tried to encourage his companion but was met with reproaches.

"You talked me into this," Leif shouted. "It's all your fault. You got me into this and you had better get me out."

On the third morning, with more than half of their rations gone, they set out again. The wind and snow had abated and, as they traveled along on their skis, their spirits rose. It was not to be for long. The wind died and the cold with it. The snow under their feet turned soggy and wet and their legs soon grew tired pushing the skis along. It was like going through a thick porridge. The snow still fell, but it was thick and wet and the atmosphere all about them was a kind of dirty yellow.

They soon began to quarrel again and not long thereafter, when they decided to turn back, Roald found that his map had become an unrecognizable sodden mass of pulp. They went on and on. Darkness fell and still the snow came down and the sogginess increased. Their feet were leaden; their muscles ached. It was a horrible space of hours that dragged on into more hours. They felt mesmerized and still they slapped along on their skis. They were afraid to stop for fear the wind would turn and they would be frozen into the slushy mass.

Finally Leif said he could no longer go on. Roald, in an attempt to encourage him, continued ahead. After a while he turned and saw his friend, far behind, sitting in the snow. He took off his pack and sleeping bag and put them down and then, with the forethought of a seasoned explorer, planted a ski stick upright next to the pack. It would be a landmark in the event of snow during the night. Then he plodded back to his friend.

Leif was close to tears. He upbraided Roald and said, "If we ever get out of this alive, I'll never talk to you again." Roald, with a wisdom astonishing in one so young, mollified him by teasing. "Come on," he said. "Cheer up. I'll let you call me crazy once we get back to town. You can tell everybody. I'll even agree with you. I'm scared too."

They decided to take a chance and rest on top of the silty snow. Amundsen went back for his sleeping bag and returned.

They crept in and soon fell fast asleep. The snow came down steadily and a nasty, thin cold crept into their very bones.

Roald was weakened by the cold and the discomfort of being soaking wet. He looked enviously at his sleeping friend and soon got an idea. He dug a hole in the snow until he found dry, crispy substance; then he crept in with his sleeping bag and soon the heat of his body and the covering gave him a sense of warmth. He fell into a deep sleep.

The dim light disturbed his slumber. It was the gray dawn. He tried to shunt it away, but he could not raise his hand. A sudden horror smote him and he was now fully awake. There above him was a cake of ice thick enough to keep him from smashing it, because he had insufficient leverage with which to raise his fist, and thin enough to show him that he was trapped. He could see upward in a bleary way. It was like a fantastic dream. And then, even while groping for a realization of what had happened to him, he recalled similar experiences of past explorers he had chanced upon in books. But this was different. This was happening to him. It was real and personal and yet, somehow, unreal.

There was a crashing sound and the edge of a ski stick came near his nose. He had no idea exactly how long he had been trapped, but he surely had lain under the ice cake for at least three hours. Oxygen began to seep down into his hole. It was Leif, of the frozen finger, who was digging him out.

Roald tried to talk but couldn't. He wanted to thank his friend, but he could only lie still and gulp air. His head was buzzing from lack of oxygen. Apparently just enough air had filtered through the crumbling ice to keep him alive.

Curiously the experience of saving his companion's life exercised a wonderful influence on Leif's spirits, for he grinned and pumped Roald's hand. Roald grinned back and they felt warm and friendly toward each other. It was a good feeling, and good for their spirits.

After Roald and Leif had rested, without words, Amundsen made his way to the ski stick which he had left in the snow to mark his pack. But the pack had disappeared.

No matter how deeply they dug, the pack apparently had sunk into the slush and been covered over by ice. Inside of Roald's pack was all their food. He no longer felt himself the seasoned and trained polar explorer. He was hungry and frightened, sick at his stomach from the icy entombing, exhausted and close to giving up. But he set his teeth, shouted at himself against the wind, recalled the perils of his heroes, and determined to give himself and Leif a fair trial before yielding. They plunged on, anxious to get away from the terrible spot and to reach, if possible, some form of shelter.

Night fell and suddenly Roald became aware that he was trudging on alone. It took effort for him to turn his head; but when he did, Leif was no longer behind him. An icefall, he said to himself. A plunge. An avalanche. A sudden drift of wet snow and sodden earth and ice over an edge of land into a declivity. He fell down on all fours, fearing the land might fall away from beneath him. When nothing happened he crept back, and heard distant cries for help. He saw a great hole and there, almost thirty feet below, was Leif trying to grapple with crumbling ice that wouldn't hold under his ice stick. He kept falling back onto his sleeping bag and starting up again, like a bug trapped inside of a smooth glass tube.

"Leif!" Roald shouted. "Leif!" He was now crying without shame. He felt his heart swelling with grief. "I got you into this," he cried. "I'll get you out. I promise I'll get you out."

Roald plunged his skis into the edge of the icefall, swiftly unknotted a ball of stout rope and tied it to the skis, and sat down in front of the skis. He got a firm seating and then wrapped his legs about the skis, which quickly had frozen into the ice. Finally he untwirled the rope, which snaked into the chasm. Leif seized hold of the rope and, using his ice stick to help himself, made his way up. His bad finger was raw and bleeding, but the blood froze quickly and the finger turned almost jet black.

Leif grinned and Roald grinned back. Again they silently pumped each other's hand. "We are men," Roald said. "We have saved a life."

They rested. Then, without a word, they began to make tracks. Dim, gray, twilighted day ran into night, and dark night ran into twilighted day. Still they plunged on, not knowing just how much time had elapsed. Actually it was four days that they went without food. Now and then they stopped for water. Here and there they found pools formed by melted snow and ice and they drank greedily. The water helped to ease the pain of cracked lips and also filled their stomachs. At times they grew faint and the snow and ice ahead of them reeled and danced endlessly. There seemed no limit to the expanse of nothingness, the waste of cold and snow and ice and craggy hills all about them. One night, like a mirage, a hut loomed before them. Blessedly the door was unlatched and they stumbled in. There was hay left over from the preceding summer. They were too fatigued to care about food. They fell into the hay and slept.

In the morning Roald awakened. Leif was in a kind of coma, half asleep and half unconscious. He tried to get him up, but there was little response other than a heavy breathing and a resentful mumbling.

Roald, estimating that they could not be far from the western edge of the plateau, set out to see if he could find the farm called Garen. He could judge from Leif's condition that, if he didn't get help and food soon, his friend might die. For an hour he made desperate tracks across the snow and suddenly he spied ski tracks on a distant ridge. He sped to them rapidly and saw they were freshly made; the wind had not yet covered them with the powdery snow.

He went up and down the hills and in the far distance, just as his breath was giving out, he saw a tiny figure. He himself began to feel dizzy and faint from lack of food. He sat down for a moment and then, summoning all his strength, raised a gigantic shout which echoed across the barren waste. He saw the figure stop, turn and wave, then begin to speed toward him.

"Who are you? What are you doing here?" the man said, pushing hard on his skis. He did not wait for an answer but followed Roald back along the trail to the hut. Once inside, he knelt and rubbed the feet of the two boys until they cried out with pain. He then gave each of them a drink from his flask. Life coursed through them and they were able to make their way, with the stranger's help, to a small farm which was not far off.

It wasn't until hours later, after Leif and he had gulped dried reindeer meat, that Roald recognized the man. He was the son-in-law of the farmer who owned Mogen, and they were almost within hailing distance of the easterly edge of the plateau from which they had set out eight days before. They had been traveling in a circle!

They were so emaciated and their eyes were so sunken in

their faces that the elderly farmer and his family could barely recognize them. The old man shook his head wonderingly. "You won't try that again for a long time," he said. "I warned you that you couldn't do it."

A year later the whole story came out. The farmer who lived on Garen, to the west, had wandered out one day to look for a sheep that had strayed away from the pen in the dead of winter. He saw ski tracks and rubbed his eyes. The tracks formed a hairpin turn. First they had come from the east and then had turned back on themselves to the east. The man marveled, for he knew that no one ever traveled across the high plain during the winter.

When Roald heard the story, he wrote to the farmer and asked him the date when he saw the ski tracks. It was as Roald had suspected! They had indeed crossed the plateau and were no more than perhaps a few hundred yards from Garen when they foolishly turned during the blizzard and retraced their steps.

When he told Leif about it, his companion on the dangerous journey said dryly, "I'm not surprised to hear it. And I wouldn't be surprised if you told me that we covered that plateau twice, coming and going. I still have nightmares in which I ski to endless places without a destination."

The experience on the plateau taught Roald several lessons. One was that good plans must be made before an expedition sets out. Another was that he had better learn navigation, and not depend on the defective compass; for had he been able to read the stars, they would not have lost their way. The third was the sharpest lesson of all: he must not take foolhardy chances when there was no need. They should have turned back the first day out from Mogen and then tried again in better weather.

He began to devour books on navigation and to make a concentrated study of all that had been written about polar expeditions and polar travel. He spoke with captains of fishing vessels, who laughed at the young man's intensity. But somehow they understood. Why else did they chance the heaving seas in their small craft for a bare living? They loved it and understood him.

From his reading and his talks at the water front Roald reached an important conclusion, one that was to make him preeminent in the world of Arctic exploration; namely, that many expedition leaders had failed because they only understand travel on land and had no knowledge of travel on sea and its hazards. Usually these leaders took along with them a sailing master who understood the sea. But this, Roald felt, meant a division of leadership responsibility. He felt that one man with a knowledge of both land and sea travel could command an expedition with some slight guarantee of success. He thus resolved to become a master seaman.

The conclusions reached by Roald at an early age—that without thorough preparation and first-rate seamanship an expedition had little or no chance of arriving at its goal— were the foremost reasons for his ultimate achievements. These two requisites, preparation and navigation, were later accepted by all Arctic explorers who followed in his wake.

In 1894 he signed on as a deck hand on a sailing ship. The men in the forecastle hooted at him when he applied himself to the skipper's books. Below decks at night, when he wasn't on watch, he read and studied by candlelight. He made a nuisance of himself questioning the mates and the captain. He tested himself by studying the stars and devoured everything he could lay his hands on about currents, wind drifts, and the great Gulf Stream. He studied depths and ways to check them and soon learned the rudiments of sails and spars and ballast.

During the day, between scrubbing decks or running up the mast to unfurl sail, he stood at the rail and watched with fascination the panorama of icebergs and floes which endlessly rose up before them and disappeared behind them and always gave way to still other processions of floating mountains of ice. He never ceased to bare his chest to the cruel winds in order to continue the hardening process he had started in his teens.

But, while they laughed, the men developed a warm affection for the "addlepate," as they called him, who wanted to be an explorer. Too, they respected his burning passion for books and knowledge and, during the long watches, they told him about many of their own experiences and filled him with hints about seafaring and braving the cold. This intercourse with older and knowledgeable men proved invaluable later on. He was often to remember this or that little trick of splicing a rope or chipping the ice from frozen sails.

During this period his personality also developed. He became less critical of men without book learning; for he found that his associates knew a great deal more than he about many things, despite the fact that they had not read or studied much. He learned to listen to and admire others and acquired the wisdom of getting the most from everyone by the use of sincere flattery.

After three years, in 1897, he felt he was ready to take the examination for a position as ship's captain, but according to the rules he had not had enough practical experience on ships to qualify for a license. However, he was fortunate enough to be referred to the Belgian Antarctic Expedition which was about to set out to study the South Magnetic Pole. Despite his youthfulness—he was only twenty-five—he was signed on as first mate.

He was beside himself with emotion, for his dream was about to take shape. The ship *Belgica* left Antwerp in late summer with Amundsen aboard. While it was known that the South Magnetic Pole is south of Australia, the ship went by way of Cape Horn—through the stormy, swirling waters at the tip of the triangle that is South America—which had been rounded by Magellan in his circumnavigation of the globe.

In late November of '97 the *Belgica* entered the Strait of Magellan and, hugging the rough coast and buffeted by the angry waters which met head on, they came to the windy and tempestuous Tierra del Fuego, one of the most desolate spots on earth. Here the South Atlantic and the South Pacific meet in gigantic swells. They were now not far from the South Pole.

The North Pole had not yet been discovered, nor had anyone reached the South Pole. None of the dozens of hardy adventurers had succeeded in negotiating the Northwest Passage.

Amundsen was now in uncharted and wild regions yet to be discovered and mapped out. He stared at the wild, gray wastes never dreaming that he was to become not only the discoverer of the South Pole but the negotiator of the Northwest Passage, nor that he was to fly over the North Pole in an airship. He had no conception of the incredible hardships, the starvation, the narrow escapes from death, and the tumult that were to become his whole life. He could not imagine that he was to become a benefactor of the human race through his contributions to man's knowledge of the world he lives in. Meanwhile he just stared at the waters.

CHAPTER III

Locked in the Ice

For a month the master of the *Belgica,* a gentle, scholarly man, lingered at Tierra del Fuego entranced by the vegetation and the rocky formations. It was the summer of the year at that latitude, though the calendar, to European eyes, spelled winter. The captain, Franz Gerlach, a Belgian, got the crew to collect and sort leaves, rock specimens, bark, and deposits made by shellfish. He also took leisurely soundings of the depths and marked them on his charts. He made detailed maps of the rugged coastline indicating inlets, small capes, tiny islands. It was a time of pleasant adventure and learning and Roald became interested in the way logbooks were kept and the manner in which scientific investigations were conducted.

More often than not, when the crew went fishing, the scientists were more anxious to study a new species, and to describe it in their notebooks, than to eat the fish. Thus the eager young man became acquainted at firsthand with how explorers combined their urge for adventure with their desire for knowledge of the world and its creatures.

He watched the scientists exclaim excitedly over a bit of seaweed that looked to him just like any other fuzzy plant. He asked questions about the strange fish of various hues and even about the barnacles which formed on the ship's hull.

One scientist in particular, Dr. Leon Perrault, was especially kind to the young man. "Look," he would say, performing an autopsy on a crab just for Roald's benefit. "You will note, please, that the breathing apparatus is somewhat different from what we find off the coast of France and Spain." And he would then proceed to explain why the apparatus was different.

It was all very pleasant; but it was dangerous, waiting and studying while winter was slowly creeping up on them. From his reading Roald knew what might be in store for the expedition. But, as a novice and first mate, he could not sound a warning for fear of being put in his place.

Finally the *Belgica* set sail due south. She passed the Shetland Islands at about the thirty-third parallel and soon came in view of the Antarctic Continent. The continent is a land mass—unlike the region about the North Pole, which is all sea and ice.

The captain set the course westward in order to chart the continental coastline, and soon the ship came into the Pacific Ocean. According to the timetable prepared at the outset of the voyage, they were now at least six months behind schedule. The *Belgica* ran rapidly under good winds and soon entered an area of fantastic icebergs where they encountered the usual gales, followed by snow and fierce, unrelenting winds.

The sailing ship, though stout, was only about two hundred tons, a fragile craft as ships are measured today. She floundered in the heavy seas and Roald, on watch, kept a rope about his middle with the two ends tied to the wheelhouse to prevent his being washed overboard. Icy waves thundered over the deck and washed through the scuppers while the ship heeled and rocked, and righted herself to Roald's surprise. She seemed to shake herself loose from the elements, dip into a vast trough as though she were being sucked into the bottomless valley of the world . . . come up again inundated with water. Soon the spars and riggings were coated with thick ice and the decks were so nearly impassable that the men had to crawl on their hands and knees in order to make their way below.

Captain Gerlach ordered the ship set about until it came under the lee side of a huge iceberg. This protected them from the wind and the heavy, pounding seas—a good tactic during a storm in more moderate climates, for a ship that can shelter itself behind a mountain or headland, on the side opposite the weather, can ride out a storm. But here things were different and the captain learned a bitter lesson.

The ship, now fairly becalmed, was riding at anchor beneath heavy swells which lifted it high up and settled it gently. The storm passed over and the exhausted men, after eating a cold supper, threw themselves into their bunks without bothering to remove their wet clothes. Roald was fast asleep when morning broke. It seemed he had been sleeping for only a moment when he heard shouting from above. His clothes were dry but stiff from salt water.

He ran up the deck. "We're in a fish bowl!" he shouted. All about the ship were mountainous icebergs. The ship was in a kind of lagoon—a quiet lagoon with no exit. Apparently, during the night, a heavy swell had cast the ship through a small barrier smack into the ring of towering ice.

The men looked at one another in fright. Now and then, as the wind changed, an iceberg would come sailing up at high speed. Fortunately it would veer. Now and then the ship, still at anchor, would swing and be threatened by two great icebergs which swerved toward it and began to behave like nut-crackers. Fortunately, too, the wind would change as it whistled through the bergs and only by a hairbreadth would the ship escape being crushed between the massive jaws of millions of tons of ice.

There was nothing they could do. There wasn't even enough room in the little bowl of water to maneuver the ship from side to side to avoid the onrushing ice mountains. This condition lasted for almost a full day. No one ate a bite of food. There was little talking as the men waited for death to come.

Toward late evening the wind changed direction; two icebergs parted and afforded a passage. The men scurried up to the sails on the swaying rope ladders. Their hands were frozen and the lines were covered with ice six inches thick.

But desperation drove them and strengthened their will. Roald threw back his head and, defying the wind, began to roar a lusty Nurse song. He shouted at the men in the riggings who were chopping away at the iced ropes with their hand axes. The boom swung about, the sails filled, and the master, himself at the wheel, made an open course through the narrow little egress of water. They sailed free.

For an hour they were happy and they sang with the elation of men who have been spared death. But then came the most terrible blow of all. The captain should have known better, but he was more of a scientist than polar expert. All about the periphery of the vast Antarctic Continent there floats a vast ring of ice that softens and hardens, that crumbles and then freezes over, depending upon the wind and the change in weather.

Had the master known this, he would have turned the prow of the ship to the north—to the safety of the open sea and freedom. Instead, bent on his purpose and knowing nothing about what was in store for him, he turned south—right into the ice pack. Before the swiftly flying vessel the pack gave and crumbled. The ship sped on through the almost loamy formation. The crew slept, ate, and talked incessantly about the time they were in the "fish bowl," as Roald had named it.

Now and then, when they glanced behind them, they saw the ice pack closing in and freezing over so that it seemed as though they were floating in a narrow lane locked off by ice.

Under the timetable they should have been wintering on the ship at the western edge of the continent—along the coast of Victoria Land. But now the lane behind them grew even narrower and the ice ahead seemed to hem them in. As the ship plowed through the icy waters the keel grated on ice and sent thumps through the vessel as though to tear it asunder. The ice got thicker and thicker and, after a week of sailing, the lane became almost impassable.

One afternoon the prow smashed into a formidably thick barrier and the ship recoiled almost as though it were being hurled backwards from a catapult. The shock was tremendout and shook the vessel from stem to stern. Roald was thrown from his berth—he had been on night watch. He raced to the deck and looked about him.

There to the south, perhaps twenty miles away, was open water. A thin skein of it, but how appealing! To the port side was nothing but thick ice. He looked at the bow side, to the north . . . nothing but ice that was rapidly closing in. The night fell and the men watched the ice creeping closer and closer. Suddenly there appeared a crack in the ice and the master ordered full sail ahead. It was a frightful mistake. Roald knew from the accounts of Arctic masters just how treacherous the shifting floes and ice barriers could be.

Forgetting for a moment that he should not criticize the captain, he shouted, "We'll be ground to bits. It's a mistake, sir."

The captain glared at him and said, "Mind your place. I give the   orders here. Moreover, I assure you that you are wrong. Get aft where you belong."

For a while Roald thought he *was* wrong. The ice crunched under the keel; the ship shook and trembled on every floe that it ran over or chopped. Then the inevitable happened. One morning the ship had no place to go. They were frozen in solid.

The officers held a consultation. The captain appeared helpless. There was one man, however, for whom Roald had formed a deep and abiding affection. This man was Dr. Frederick Cook, the ship's physician, whose later life was to be bitter and tragic. Without him, Amundsen says, the ship could not have been saved. And in later years, true to his personal courage, Roald never abandoned his trust in the man who, because he claimed to have reached the North Pole, was called a charlatan and a liar and later spent many years in the federal prison at Fort Leavenworth for perpetrating swindles in oil stocks.

"I want you to be my right-hand man," Dr. Cook said. "You have more sense than most of us, I guess, because you have done a great deal of reading. Moreover, you appear to be applying what you've read to good advantage. You have a good head for observation on your shoulders."

Dr. Cook, aided by young Amundsen, took over during the "emergency," as it was called for the moment.

The emergency however, lasted for thirteen months, during which they were held fast in a block of ice that spread for hundreds upon hundreds of miles on every side. They were lost in a sea of ice fields, hunger, cold, despair, misery, illness, insanity, and hatred. But Dr. Cook and Amundsen finally managed to get them back to safety.

CHAPTER IV

From the Basement to the Ceiling

For thirteen months they were icebound, fixed and frozen in a vast nothingness of dazzling white. For more than a year the men, living close together and hopeless, either formed warm attachments or developed intense dislikes for one another. Under the stress of not knowing if and when they would die, emotions ranged high. Their uneasiness knew no bounds. They never were comfortable; they never had enough to eat; they never knew what the next day would bring. They began thinking of their homes and felt they would never see their loved ones again, even though they had expected to be gone for several years.

Because they were lost, the men felt sure the world considered them lost. And in the white waste they quarreled, starved, hated, liked, cooperated, planned crazy stunts, read and reread, concocted games to ward off boredom, and felt a revulsion for the ice about them even though they learned to accept it.

Mornings and evenings Roald, Dr. Cook, and Dr. Perrier

met by agreement on deck or on the ice and tried to bolster one another's morale.

"It's like living in an insane asylum," Dr. Cook said.

They laughed but it was not merry laughter. They compared notes about the crew and wondered who would be the first to go beserk.

"I nominate the captain," Roald said.

The two mentors laughed. "He is too tired to go crazy," Cook suggested. Again they laughed. And the laughter, brittle as it was, did them good.

"It's peculiar, being the only sane persons on a lunatic ship asylum, isn't it, sir?" Roald said.

Through it all the ship stood up and was not crushed as the ice thickened all around it. The men grew beards and Amundsen developed a fine, square spade set of which he was quite proud. His cheeks became sunken and his eyes merely squinted. His tall, rangy figure grew more gaunt and he tried to recall what other explorers had done in similar situations. Throughout the ordeal his friend Dr. Cook helped him, taught him, encouraged him, and took him on forages across the vast ice fields to keep him from developing the inertia and coma that lead to insanity or death.

An inventory was taken. It was poor indeed. For one thing, not enough warm clothing had been provided—simply because under the timetable only four men were supposed to stay on the icy continent, while the ship was to go north to warmer waters. There was not enough oil and tallow for light. There was not enough food. And of course, in those days, there was no radio.

Inside of three months one sailor, a Frenchman named Ernest Poulson, appeared on deck one morning raving-mad.

He was carrying a knife and he attacked all those about him. Then he leaped over the side and sped across the ice. He ran and ran until he fell. Roald sped after the sailor, while Dr. Cook treated the wounds of those who had been attacked. But the sailor was dead when Roald reached him. They hacked out a place in the ice and buried him. Then they raised the French flag above his grave.

The men were frightened and sobered when the burial was over. No man looked at another and there was fear in everyone's eyes.

Before they got back to the ship, Dr. Cook climbed atop a hummock and called for attention. "Men," he said, "we're going through a bad time. I am sure that with enough thought and planning we'll get out of it. But we must maintain level heads. We must be strong. Strong," he repeated. "Otherwise we will all die." Then he turned to Roald and commanded, "Sing!"

Roald broke out into a Norwegian sea chantey, the kind that has dozens of verses. The men joined him and for a time there reigned a sense of comfort and peace. But it was not to last very long.

Two weeks later a second sailor suddenly climbed the mast, shouted "Open water," and plunged to his death

"Hallucinations," said Dr. Cook. Again there was a burial.

The men looked at the two flags several hundred yards away and the sight seemed to unnerve them. Dr. Cook noticed this, and one night he and Roald made their way across the flinty snow and ice and moved the flags over a hummock where they could not be seen by the crew. They could not dig up the bodies, which were frozen solid; but they knew the signs of the miniature graveyard should be removed.

The crew, immersed in its own personal problems of cold and hunger, did not appear to notice a thing. Dr. Cook smiled at Roald, and Roald smiled back.

Then scurvy struck. The lack of Vitamin C and fresh foods gave the men terrible toothaches and stomach ailments. Two others died . . . and that night two more French flags were shifted over the hummock of ice out of sight. The master took to his bed and so did Roald and Cook.

"We must have fresh meat or we will die, all of us," Cook said. At first he and Amundsen tried to fish in the ice; but even when they did manage to make a hole large enough to drop a line into, the ice would freeze over rapidly and snag the project. "I don't even know if there is any fish here," Cook said.

"The fish are probably hibernating," Roald said. "Who knows, there may be specimens here which freeze in for the winter. It may be a custom of the country."

"If you keep your humor," Cook said, "you will be a great explorer and leader. Don't forget it."

Roald glowed.

So they took their harpoons and guns and went out across the ice fields. Not far off, there were friendly penguins resembling head waiters with their white vests, courteous manners, and waddling steps. They were easy to kill, although Roald felt a sense of remorse. "I feel as though I'm betraying their trust," he said.

"If they like us, they should be glad to help us out," said Cook, batting one of the penguins over the head with a short club.

The crew devoured the penguin meat. While the flavor was rather poor and the flesh somewhat oily, it did them good; for the oil contains the vitamins necessary to good digestion and health. Soon Roald and Cook began to spend exhausting days foraging the fields in search of seals basking on ice floes. These died hard and were difficult to drag back to the ship. However, out of timber lashed together, the pair were able to make a kind of sled and they brought back hundreds of pounds of seal flesh.

The men brightened at the sight of the meat. One of them seized a great side of seal and danced about with it. Cook glanced at Roald, who took the hint. "Come on," he shouted. "I'm going to be the best seal chef below the Equator."

The master refused to eat any of the penguin or seal meat. "It all tastes rancid and it's not fit for a human being," he said. "I forbid anyone to eat it." Roald and Cook paid no attention to him but broiled or boiled the meat, drank the soup and ate the meat. The crew followed suit and soon the men were out of danger of scurvy. Roald had boils and stomachaches, but he knew he was hardy and he waited for the meat and soup to heal him. Soon he was well.

The captain, seeing how much better his men were, deigned to taste the soup and eat some of the meat and he picked up so rapidly that he withdrew his censorship.

Once the kill of meat became larger than the consumption, Roald built a kind of icebox, a cairn of ice, under which he buried the meat for future use. Thus, when storms howled across the plains, it was a simple matter to go out to the cache, back through the ice, and drag out several buried seal steaks weighing fifty pounds or more.

With a bowlful of hot seal fat in his stomach and a thick lump of penguin meat in his fist, Roald lay in his bunk reading and munching. The fat was also used in improvised lamps which stank dreadfully but were long-lasting. Sometimes he threw back his head and shouted at nothing at all, happy to be alive and living the life of the explorer. The men thought he was going crazy, but he paid no attention to them and continued to study the books and charts which he had reread countless times.

At last the long Antarctic night came imperceptibly to an end. The soft but impenetrable darkness turned shadowy and gray and on some days there was even a glimmering of light. Soon, before they became aware of it, there were almost definite demarcations between light and darkness, and a gladness or a kind of hope came to the men. This was reflected in conversation, whereas before there had been little talk; and in gaiety, where before there had been none at all. The entombed crew began to feel that perhaps something would now happen.

One day Roald noticed a spot of blue on the ice, almost a mile distant. With the passing hours the blue grew more distinct and even widened. He rubbed his eyes, but it was no trick of sun, ice, or vision. The blueness became water and he shouted. The men came running. "Water," they shouted, "water!"—like men in the hot desert.

Cook and Roald trekked over the ice and examined the water. They went to the brink and felt it. It was ocean water, cold and briny. They ascended a hill and tried to trace the flow of it. And it appeared to flow endlessly, far to the horizon. But the ice they were on was thick and immovable.

"The ice will soon break up," said the master. But the men would not wait. Cook said that in his considered judgment it would be from two to three months before the ice barrier between them and the blue waters would break up and allow them to sail free. However, he had a plan.

It was a mad and almost savage plan in that it embraced fantastic toil by men who had been weakened by the rigors of a year on ice and without solid nourishment. Moreover, there wasn't enough warm clothing to go around so that the entire crew could work in unison. Cook, backed by Amundsen, pushed for his plan and Roald, remembering his reading about other icebound explorers, whipped out a huge needle and shouted, "I will make clothes." He set to work at once.

On the deck he had the ship's carpenter cut several dozen red blankets into baggy suits that resembled the nightclothes worn by children—long arms, long feet, loose and shapeless bodies.

"Dress," Amundsen commanded when the cutting and sewing were done. The crew dressed, looked at one another, and burst into hysterical laughter. They roared and roared until they were rolling on the deck. It was a theatrical sight, as if the cast of a musical comedy had suddenly appeared against a backdrop of glaciers dressed in firemen's-red sleeping suits. Penguins, attracted by the laughter and the shouting, waddled over to have a better look. Amundsen said, "Look. The first row, all dressed up in dress suits, is watching us perform."

The haggard men in the bright, warm clothing went over the side on planks. Several, weakened by scurvy and despair, had not been on the ice for months. Others had refused to take an interest in anything, so debilitated were they in spirit and in the will to live. The long months had taken a terrible toll.

Each man was armed with what could be found. One had an ax, another a cleaver, a third a ski stick, a fourth a pick, a fifth just a file, and so on. These were pitiful objects with which to attack thousands of tons of ice, perhaps ten feet thick and stretching for almost a mile to the blue waters. But Cook, who took charge, began to formulate his plan. It was a simple one: "Chop and dig the ice into cakes." The men went at it with a will, but after fifteen minutes most of them refused to go on. "This is impossible," they said. But Cook and Roald, working with a will, paid them no heed. Soon, out of shame, the men continued.

They hacked and hacked and jabbed and jabbed and filed and stomped. They drove long pegs into the ice and dislodged great chunks. These floated away and soon, on the first day, there was more than two yards of clear water before them—with almost fourteen hundred yards to go. But it was a start. The men felt better for the exercise and the fresh air, and went to sleep elated and exhausted. The next morning Cook, who was out early on deck, became sick at heart. During the night their little clearing in the ice had become solidly frozen over.

But he would not despair. While the men looked on silently, he and Roald set explosive charges in the sections that had been made the day before. "This can't be as frozen as the untouched sections," Roald said. "After all, it was only overnight that the ice cakes came together."

The blasts were set and touched off and the cakes broke apart and floated. The men cheered, donned their Red Riding Hood costumes, and went to work again. It was back-breaking.

For almost a month, from the thin dawn to early nightfall, they labored. Roald set charges at the ends of the cakes before he went to sleep. All he had to do was to touch them off in the morning and the cakes would break asunder.

It became a nightmare on ice. The grueling work began to

tell on the men; but they continued, for the instinct for survival is an imperishable urge. They drove their spikes; they hammered and smashed. They cut and sawed; they sought out cracks and drove in skis and hammered them. And slowly, slowly, the thin channel became a reality. Even the ill and dispirited skipper was in high spirits.

But the next morning the great ice pack had moved in and sealed the channel tightly. All their work had been in vain.

A gigantic Dane, who had swung his ax tirelessly day after day without stopping, advanced on Roald. "You liar," he said. "I'm going to take your head off." He swung the ax and Dr. Cook stepped forward. "You have terrible blisters on your hand that I must look at," he said quietly. The Dane stared for a moment and then broke into laughter. Roald laughed and the crew laughed. "I guess we'll eat penguin for another year. I'm beginning to like it," Roald said. Again the men laughed.

For two days the ice pack held. Then the wind shifted, and there was their lagoon—the narrow strip of water they had hacked out with so much toil—blue, sparkling in the sun, and inviting.

There were shouted commands—ropes were hitched to the *Belgica;* the men grabbed them, placed them over their shoulders, and heave-hoed with might and main. The good and patient ship, which had not moved an inch for more than a year, groaned, strained, and then, with a crashing of tired timbers, floated free and seemed actually to dance on the waters. Again a cheer went up. Most of the men cried to see her afloat. A ship becomes a dear thing to men who work her and live on her. No one laughed at the tears.

Roald, unashamed of his tears, walked over and patted her

flanks. "Good to be in motion again, hah?" he asked. It was a moment he never forgot.

The *Belgica* was literally dragged into the open waters and then the men clambered aboard. But a new peril awaited them.

The sails, which had been sewn and repaired days before, swelled with the wind. The ship heeled, took a course, and the wheel sent her responding lightly and easily as though she were glad to be at the beck of the steersman. But there, looming before them, were two huge icebergs like sentinels barring their path to the open sea which lay just ahead. The channel between the bergs was so narrow that it seemed the ship would surely be scraped down to her last inch if she tried to pass through.

"Let's make a run for it," the captain shouted.

"No," cried Roald. "Those bergs will crush us if the wind shifts, or they will shave us into nothing if we veer just an inch."

Cook stepped in with an idea. He ran below and came up with dozens of sealskins he had saved for coats. "Let's lash these over the sides," he urged, and they followed his suggestion. The device saved the ship and the men.

Slowly, slowly, with Roald at the wheel, the ship made her way under light sail. There was a crashing sound as sections of the icebergs skimmed the bottom of the *Belgica* and scraped her sides. There was moaning and groaning as the wind tugged at the sails while the hard ice, on either side, tried to hold the ship in check. At times the *Belgica* shook as though she were about to be torn to shreds. Intense cold set in and the sun was almost blotted out as the ship with the silent crew made her way between the mountainous bergs.

At one point the ship heeled away over as a berg rocked in the wind and caught her below the waterline. The ship bobbed, righted, and leaned the other way. Roald steered as though the wheel alone would take them through the long pass. The cold grew even more intense. It must have been at least thirty degrees below zero. Roald, bare to the waist and shouting though he did not know it, was unaware of the bite. His beard was matted with ice and his nostrils were thick with frozen mucus. At one point he lost his left glove and his hand stuck to the wheel. He tore it away from the icy mucilage and lost several inches of skin. The hand bled and the blood froze.

He shouted over his shoulder. "Full sail!" The men clambered and set sail. The sails filled, there was a rending crash, the sealskins were ripped off the sides, and the *Belgica,* scarred and scratched and gouged on both sides, floated free in the Pacific Ocean. The endless frozen-in time of thirteen months was over. The men danced, kissed one another, apologized for quarreling, and the doctor brought out his medicine chest with several bottles of spirits. Even the seal and penguin stew, boiled in ice water, tasted good for a change.

The captain, not wishing to give credit to Cook for fear of losing face, approached Roald in the presence of the men and congratulated him. "That was a splendid job you did, my boy," he said.

Roald rose to the occasion. He did not wish to embarrass the captain but, at the same time, he didn't for a moment want to take credit from Dr. Cook. So he said diplomatically, "I was just the brawn and Dr. Cook was the brains. I believe brains are more important when men are in trouble than brawn."

Cook, standing offside, smiled. Later he said to Roald, "You did very well by me and you are an honest man."

Roald replied, "I don't think dishonesty can ever get men out of danger, sir."

"That's a stuffy statement, in a way," Cook responded. "But it has a lot of meat to it."

For days they sailed not knowing where they were going. During the passage between the two bergs, the ship's chronometer had been broken and they had only the stars to guide them on a northerly course.

One morning the man on the crow's-nest raised the immemorial cry of "Land ho!"

There lay Church Island, so called because of its cathedral-like pillars, rocks, and hummocks rising steeply from the tiny isle. Now at last they could get their bearings. Now they could sail for home. But for several months the stout ship, which had negotiated such bad passage, plowed its way through dangerous straits and skirted lofty icebergs. It was two years, all told, before Amundsen returned home to his native Norway.

He was much older than his twenty-seven years. He had learned much, had suffered much. The one great adventure on the *Belgica* would have sufficed another man for an entire lifetime. But not Amundsen. "I am just whetted," he told his friends.

He strode the streets of Oslo, tall, rangy, with his skin as deeply wind-bitten as some craggy rock on an Arctic promontory. Indeed one of his friends said that he looked like walking proof of the theory of rock erosion.

He ran into his old friend Leif and they spent many an evening together talking about the voyage to the Antarctic.

Leif, by this time, was married and had a child. "I envy you," he said sadly. "I love my wife and our baby, but it would be nice to be young and venturesome again."

Roald stared at him in amazement. "Do you think going on adventures is a monopoly of youth? Or do you think it marks a man as being young?"

Leif thought for a moment. "It's not a matter of age. It's a matter of youthful spirit. I think back often to our exploit on the plateau. It was you who got us through. Not me. You will always be the youthful adventurer, I think."

Amundsen continued his studies with the skimpy sums at his disposal and soon took the examination for a master's license. Holding this license proudly in his hand, he sought out Dr. Fridtjof Nansen, the dean of explorers, zoologist, and future statesman. Nansen, who had ranged widely in the Arctic regions and had charted many islands and seas, did not laugh at the earnest young man.

"It is a hard life. There are few rewards you will gain in your lifetime except a smattering of fame among those who don't understand. You may lose your life because of one misstep. You will not perhaps know the joys of having a wife and children. If you do decide to marry, you will be doing a good woman a great injustice; for you will never be home and she will not know for years whether or not you are dead.

"But if this is what you want"—and here he looked into Roald's luminous eyes—"this is what you want. I pity you, envy you, and give you my blessings. Hit the top and the bottom of the world. Make them your empires even though you will never rule over them. And here is my commendation in letter form." The great man then wrote a warm note to those who might best help Amundsen become a leader on his own.

Roald walked out on a cloud. The world's uncharted regions seemed close at hand, within his grasp. He wondered why he was driven to chart them and he had a long talk with himself that night.

"Why do I want to do this?" he asked himself. There was no answer. "Am I a compass that points to the north? Is there some kind of magnetic attraction inside of me? Why don't I get a respectable job, settle down and get married, and have a life of warmth, ease, and comfort?" But there was no answer at all. He shrugged, had a cup of coffee after walking the streets all night, and reconciled himself to the fact that he was a haunted man. "Haunted by icy ghosts," he said to himself. Then he went ahead to follow through on the great man's letters.

But Dr. Nansen's recommendations did not take hold in all quarters. Amundsen applied for a job at the British Observatory at Kew, explaining that he wished to continue his studies in the science of magnetism and in magnetic observations. His offer to work for nothing was turned down. However, following one lead after another, he finally landed a post at the Deutsche Seewärte in Hamburg, Germany—but only after an amusing and instructive interview with George von Neumayer, the director of the famous observatory.

The kindly old man looked at him and asked gently, "Why do you want to study here?"

"I want to be an explorer. I already have a master's license and I have been for two years in the Antarctic."

The director shook his head pityingly. "That's a strange whim, my son."

"But I also want to find the Northwest Passage," Amundsen blurted out.

The astronomer nodded. "There must be something else."

Amundsen thought feverishly. He almost fled from the room upon realizing how foolish he must sound. Then he had an idea and used it as a desperate measure.

"I want to locate the North Magnetic Pole. That is my reason for wanting to work under you."

The man with the small body and the great shock of white hair ran to him and embraced him. "That is the great adventure, the Magnetic Pole. Find that and you will be mankind's benefactor."

Not only did the old man teach him a great deal but he fed him well in high, old German fashion. Amundsen to the end of his life never forgot those meals and often, when he was chewing his dog's harness, he thought of those bumper roasts and thick, savory gravies with potato dumplings.

He worked hard and grew even leaner, despite the old man's frequent invitations to dinner. He then went on to study in Potsdam and at the famed Wilhelmstrasse observatory in Berlin.

Here he came to the notice of several underpaid but illustrious scientists. One of them, Dr. Otto Erhardt, gave him a great deal of time. "Just because you are a madman, I will help you," the elderly weather expert said. "Only a madman would wish to spend his life at unrewarding pursuits. You will be great after you are dead. But meantime you will have a fascinating and poverty-stricken life."

Roald laughed. "I am a madman and so are you, Herr Professor. I say this with deepest respect. You, as well, have spent your life on things people don't as yet appreciate."

"They will. They will," Dr. Erhardt said. "If you live long enough, you will see how important the outer spaces will become to the people of the world. In aviation. In charting the weather for ships at sea and for industry. During war and in peace. Just wait."

So Roald studied and learned. Between times he took odd jobs and saved as much money as he could. In 1900, when he felt he was ready to sail on his own, he made a down payment on a small, forty-seven-ton vessel that had seen almost twenty-seven years of service as a fishing boat in the North Atlantic.

He looked upon the boat as a good omen, for it was exactly his own age. He stroked its smelly cords and sides and went down on his hands and knees and scrubbed and scrubbed. It was in frightful condition, but he loved it because it was all his own—all, that is, except for a few more payments.

For the next two years he worked at various jobs, even becoming a waiter in water-front restaurants to keep himself and the boat alive. Now and then he inveigled a crew into taking exploratory cruises with him in the ship, which he named the *Gjoa*. Once he went almost as far as Greenland and began to know and understood the feel of the small vessel, how it behaved under stormy conditions, how it stood up to a beating. He became one with the old fishing boat and tended her carefully as a prize possession.

At times he took a few of his coworkers or friends down to the ship and showed them around. He plunged below into the galley and, ducking his head, led them through the line of berths. He showed them the good wood in the hull and encouraged them to climb the mast.

"You are in love with your ship," one of his friends said

wisely. "I guess I am," Amundsen said gravely. And so he was. He breathed the ship; he thought of it when he ate and he dreamed about it when he slept. Nothing else excited him. He spent his waking days on board. When he was not aboard, he was studying books or navigation charts at the library.

Once again he had a long conference with himself. "What kind of man am I? Why am I different from all other men I know?" He could not find any answer at all. A librarian to whom he spoke said that he must descend from a long line of Vikings. "That is why you seek the sea, the polar sea. It must be in your blood and it is a call from your ancestors."

Amundsen, the realist, would have none of this "psychic reasoning," as he called it. "I guess I just like cold weather," he said with humor. But his heart knew better. And still he could never answer the question he had within himself. Likely it is one which no man of adventurous spirit can answer.

He planned to take off late in 1902, but creditors hounded him for payment. He needed money for supplies and for the crew, and to pay off the balance due on the ship. He begged all kinds of societies to help him. But to no avail. He hounded rich men and offered to name continents after them. But they, as well, turned a deaf ear to his promises of immortality. "What is a silly island named after me in the Far North?" they said to him. "What would it mean to me? Is it worth all that money?" He could not even convince them that he would succeed in finding an unknown island to name after them.

On June 15 he was presented with a bailiff's bill which threatened him with lawsuit and the seizure of his ship and supplies unless he paid off.

But he was a man with a mission and could not be turned from his destiny. He got supplies on credit, poured dulcet words into the ears of a crew, obtained new spars and ropes, painted the *Gjoa* and went aboard. He was not a day too soon.

That evening, in a frightful rainstorm, he and seven crewmen, excited over the adventure, cut loose from the pier, set the sails and, at midnight, quietly and slowly made their way toward the North Sea bent on finding the Northwest Passage.

The men stayed up all night laughing at the discomfiture of the tradesmen who would come to the wharf in the morning to seize the vessel and everything aboard.

By that time Amundsen and his doughty little ship were standing out to sea embarked on a history-making cruise.

CHAPTER V

The Mad, Lucky Viking

When Ferdinand Magellan's expedition circumnavigated the globe early in the sixteenth century, the fact was definitely established, even to the most skeptical, that the world was round. The four-year voyage, during which Magellan himself was killed in a battle with natives, also proved that there was a vast land surface, the Americas, lying between the Atlantic and the Pacific Oceans.

Throughout the centuries, dozens of explorers, including Christopher Columbus, tried to find a water route across the Americas in order to facilitate trade with the Far East. Time and again these expeditions failed. There was to be no short and easy way until the opening of the Panama Canal, which took ten years to build and was completed in 1914.

But adventurers, not knowing this, tried again and again and failed. Among them were Henry Hudson, who sailed into the Arctic and discovered Hudson Bay; Martin Frobisher, who discovered Frobisher Sound; Captain Robert McClure, of the British Navy, who in 1853 was forced to abandon His Majesty's ship *Investigator* at Mercy Bay while exploring Banks Island in search of another British expedition, led by

Sir John Franklin, that perished in search of the Northwest Passage.

Franklin's party of one hundred and five men aboard the vessels *Erebus* and *Terror* was lost sometime between 1845 and 1848, though its fate was not determined until 1854.

Captain McClure's group spent two winters at Mercy Bay in the hope of rescue by relief ships. Thrown on their own resources, the men crossed the strait to Melville Island by sledge in June of 1853 and were rescued by relief ships at Winter Harbor.

In 1850 McClure had penetrated Prince of Wales Strait to within thirty miles of its exit into Melville Sound. Other navigators followed him trying to find a passage through McClure Strait, which had been discovered by the doughty captain.

Amundsen had a vast collection of literature on the subject of the Northwest Passage which he had purchased in London. One book, written by Admiral Sir Leopold McClintock, hammered away at the theory that, if a clear passage from the Atlantic to the Pacific existed, it would be found far south of the routes taken by other expeditions.

When Amundsen in his little *Gjoa* set sail toward Skagerrak and the North Sea, he knew full well he was embarking on an adventure that had ended in disaster for many expeditions far better than his. To date, the man who had gone farther than any other explorer in trying to negotiate the Passage was Sir Allen Young, who in his *Pandora* had reached an almost halfway point when he found himself blocked by shallow waters, icebergs, and land masses.

It is difficult to believe that great sections of the world were still uncharted as recently as 1903, when the *Gjoa* headed east. It remained for Amundsen to fit in the two remaining pieces of the world's jigsaw puzzle: the Northwest Passage, which he discovered when he was only thirty-three years old, and later the South Pole, which in effect he put on the map.

As a matter of fact, it was not until August of 1954 that two United States icebreakers, the Navy's *Burton Island* and the Coast Guard's *Northwind,* crashed their way through a shorter route than Amundsen had found. The ships, on a joint United States and Canadian expedition carrying scientists who were conducting hydrographic and oceanographic surveys in the Beaufort Sea and McClure Strait, negotiated the shorter passage by main force and by accident.

The *Burton Island,* under the command of Everett A. Trickey, smashed through the middle of McClure Strait east to west and then cut back west to east along the northern edge of the ice-locked Passage. McClure Strait, far beyond the Arctic Circle, lies between Melville Island and Banks Island and connects Viscount Melvile Sound with the Arctic Ocean. Captain William L. Maloney, who commanded the *Northwind,* entered the Strait from the Arctic Ocean and made his way along the southern edge from west to east.

This feat by the two powerful icebreakers utilizing magnificent engines was hailed by the world press. The success thus makes Amundsen's adventure and his negotiation of the Passage in his tiny *Gjoa* all the more astounding. The icebreakers were two hundred and sixty-nine feet long, while the *Gjoa* was barely seventy feet.

The *Gjoa* bounced along on the stormy North Atlantic, but the men were of good cheer. They had been carefully selected by Amundsen, who from his experiences in the Antarctic had learned to judge men by the fire in them. They had to have a boyish sense of adventure and a maturity of judgment, both at the same time. These were rare qualities, but Roald recognized them when he saw them.

Several scientists had volunteered to go along on the voyage, but Amundsen, bolstered by his training at the observatories, resolved to be his own expert. Over a period of several months he obtained excellent advice from Nansen and others as to the kind of scientific equipment to take along. Too, he spent every conceivable moment reading up on the best ways of utilizing these instruments. Various scientific societies begged him to observe and take notes on such phenomena as wild life in the North, Arctic grasses, and the tides. These groups were not so well supported financially as they are today and they could give him no subsidy with which to purchase the necessary equipment, which was quite expensive. However, as he said, "I managed somehow to obtain good credit mainly because people were startled when they saw how young I was."

His courses in navigation stood him in good stead and, despite the howling gales for which the North Atlantic is famous, it wasn't long before they reached the port of Godhavn on Disko Island, which lies west of the great Greenland land mass. There they replenished their supplies out of their meager funds, took on water, and purchased on credit a score of good Husky dogs from the Royal Danish Trading Company. Amundsen chuckled at obtaining the credit. "Apparently news of our creditors on the dock back home hasn't as yet reached these shores," he said.

The little ship, now crowded to its very deck with supplies so that it looked more like a barge than a vessel, headed due north. Actually the ship was imperiled by its cargo, which weighed it down almost to the waterline. But Amundsen, with a calculating eye, took the long gamble that they would not founder.

When they ran into frightful squalls, fogs, roaring winds, and smashing ice that threatened to pulverize the almost unmanageable ship, the men complained bitterly about the overloading. They begged him to cast loose the heavy crates which were lashed on the deck. But the captain held firm. "We will need the supplies. Without them we may as well go back."

They turned west at Melville Bay, north of Baffin Bay and inside the great hook of Greenland. Here they ran into what is considered to be one of the worst bodies of water in the world. Indeed Melville Bay is called "the graveyard of ships," for hundreds of vessels and fishing smacks have foundered and been sunk in the unrelenting fury that lashes the area. The *Gjoa* was just a cockleshell in a basin of turbulence.

Some of the crew begged the captain to seek shelter or, better, to withdraw from Melville Bay. "I will not," he said. "I'll get all of you through. Rely upon me. Best of all, rely upon the *Gjoa*. I understand her and she understands me. We're the same age, you know."

Amundsen's seamanship, along with a sort of sixth sense that made him sensitive to every roll and heave of the ship, stood him in good stead. For without it the ship would have gone down. The vessel yawed and swung, skipped and banged into the troughs of the great waves; then it rose with incredible speed on the top of another wave only to bang and smash down again into the next trough.

He stood at the tiller for three days and three nights, refusing to surrender it to any of the company. "The responsibility is mine," he shouted in the gale. It was here that he developed his reputation for being a "cold and frosty man, an unapproachable man." He was anything but that. Intrinsically he was very shy and reserved. But under hardship and duress he felt responsibility and the need to be a man and to take over full command. He could not alow the crew to see the joy with which he faced the challenge of the seas and the over-laden ship. He loved it and ordered the men below so that he could shout into the wind, yell at the great waves, and pat the *Gjoa's* tiller as though it were a beloved dog.

Like some Viking of old, when the wind screamed he screamed above it. When tons of water cascaded over the sides and the boat stood on its head, he lashed himself to the tiller with a stout rope and thundered his defiance. He declared later that he must have been a mad sight, his beard matted with ice, his chest bare to the elements, and his arms working like pistons to hold the ship on its course.

At last they rounded Cape York and pushed to Dalrymple Rock, where they made a landing. There they took on more supplies, including barrels of gasoline for the small auxiliary motor with which the *Gjoa* was fitted. The men were worried about fire hazards, for gasoline was then a new thing. The barrels were lashed on deck and the vessel took off for Beechy Island, north of North Somerset Island, where Amundsen planned to set up a station for magnetic observations.

Scientists of course knew exactly where the North Pole was, though no one, as yet, had been there. On the nautical maps of the world it was pinpointed at the northern end of the earth's axis at latitude ninety degrees and longtitude zero. But the North Magnetic Pole was another matter. For centuries, since the compass came into use, it had been known that the needle does not point to the true north but somewhat away from it. This had always puzzled scientists, for the freely suspended magnetic needle, while pointing always in the general direction of the North Pole, is always off by some degrees. Too, mariners had observed that the needle did not always seem to point exactly to the same spot but shifted now and then if ever so slightly.

Amundsen was determined not only to find the Northwest Passage, the chief project of the expedition, but to try and locate the Magnetic Pole. For the latter, he had on board delicate scientific recording instruments. In order to assure that these instruments would not be affected by iron, which can influence their readings, every nail on the ship and in the crates was made of copper, which is nonmagnetic. Though the copper nails were very expensive, Amundsen knew they were mandatory.

Beechy Island was a drab, lonely, forsaken place. Here the instruments were set up and, after a few days, Amundsen noted in his log that the Magnetic Pole, from his findings, was located on the west coast of a jut of land called Boothia Felix. Fascinatingly enough, observations made as recently as 1953 indicate that the North Magnetic Pole is at 73°35′ N. lat., 92°20′ W. long., not too far away from Amundsen's own observations made with inferior equipment.

They now embarked and made Peel Strait, the farthest point yet reached by any explorer seeking the Passage. Sir Allen Young, who had come this far in his *Pandora,* had made soundings of depths to this point. Beyond was uncharted land, and water fraught with danger from ice, shallow depths, and reefs. To all purposes the *Gjoa* and her complement, from here on, might have been traversing an area on another planet, for no one had ever set sail or foot in the unexplored region. Mystery lay ahead and the men were thrilled.

Suddenly there was a crash and a grating sound. The *Gjoa's* sails flapped, but the ship was held fast by an invisible clutch below. There was a rending sound, then a bump and another crash. The ship was now held in a vise.

The men scampered below to see if a hole had been torn in the keel. "Not a drop of water," they reported cheerfully. Amundsen could not believe it. Again they went below and said there were no holes. It seemed like a miracle. Now came the problem of getting the ship afloat again.

For seven hours they stuck fast. Like the responsible skipper he was, Amundsen went over the stores to see how much food they had and he calculated how long it would take for the heavy seas to pound the *Gjoa* into splinters. There was no chance of rescue even if they could have communicated with the outside world. There was nothing to do but wait for death to overtake them. Meantime Amundsen set about constructing a raft, to which he lashed food and a keg of water in the event they should founder.

The men followed his orders grimly. There was a dead silence as they prepared for destruction. What difference if they floated helplessly on an icy sea or were dashed to pieces? Either way meant death, one more lingering than the other.

A sailor asked the captain whether he would lead them in prayer. They gathered on deck and, with the sea lashing about them, Amundsen opened the Bible at random. By mere chance his finger fell on the Book of Isaiah, chapter 3.

As he said later, goose pimples rose on his skin as he read: "For, behold, the Lord, the Lord of hosts, doth take away from Jerusalem and from Judah the stay and the staff, the whole stay of bread, and the whole stay of water."

It is the chapter about the confusion that results from sin and the presumption of the people.

"I know we are all sinners," he said to his crew. "But may God help us." It was a stirring sight, the men standing bareheaded on the deck and hearing the trumpeting words of the great Prophet as though they were a personal message.

"I've never forgotten that moment," Amundsen said in later years on lecture tours. "Men who lead dangerous lives invariably call upon God, for He is at the North Pole and the South Pole. I never forgot that moment and I never failed to pray whenever I was in distress. For help came almost immediately."

There was a terrific heave and the ship broke free as a great wave lifted it over the reef. Dawn was just breaking in the murky sky when they came afloat. A man went over the side on a little platform to see what damage had been caused. "The rudder, the rudder!" he cried. When the ship had scraped off the rock, the rudder had been pushed upwards and the pins which held it at the top and bottom were about to slide out of the metal rings in which they rested. They had emerged from one danger only to plunge into another.

Amundsen sprang to the tiller. The rudder did not respond. The wheel spun uselessly. "It is disengaged," he cried. "There's no movement." Carefully, barely daring to breathe, they watched the pins and the rudder. Were the rudder to be cast loose, they would float helplessly in the stormy waters, at the mercy of the winds, and be dashed against the rocks.

A wave came up—and up came the pins a bit more, edging out of the rings. Up came the rudder as well. Another wave, and the pins were barely in their sockets. Another, and one of the pins began to lean over. There was nothing to do. Suddenly, as the *Gjoa* yawed helplessly, a wave came broadside, heeled the ship over, and with a thump the pins settled into their rings. Amundsen twirled the wheel—and the *Gjoa* responded.

"I've never heard a more satisfactory sound in my life than that thump," Amundsen said. The men laughed. They had rarely heard levity in their captain's speech. They began to regard him as the luckiest man they'd ever known. "If that wave had come from the other direction, the pins would have fallen out," one said to him. "On the sea we never use the word 'if,' simply because it has no use," the captain said sternly.

One day later, destruction threatened them again. The heavy smell of gasoline, some of which had been stored near the little auxiliary motor, came sifting up to the deck. An investigation was made and they found that one of the barrels was leaking. Amundsen ordered the engineer to pump the gasoline out of that barrel into another.

The boat made its way to a small island, for night was falling. They were about to anchor when the dread cry of "Fire!" screamed across the deck.

The men were paralyzed with fear. The cry of "Fire!" in the days of wooden ships was the most frightful that could arise at sea. One man rushed to the rail and was about to fling himself overboard when Amundsen, with a giant stride, swung his fist and knocked him to the deck. "Anybody else want to go overboard?" he turned and asked. The panic passed and the men waited quietly for instructions. The man who was knocked down got up and rubbed his ear. "That's a thick ear you gave me, captain," he said. "That's because I wanted it to go with your thick head," Amundsen said. "Now let's get to work," he snapped.

Great tongues of flame came licking up from the engine room below. The hatch was opened and they looked down into an inferno. Cracking out orders, Amundsen ran to the fire buckets and the men dipped water from over the side and kept pouring it into the bowels of the ship. The battle lasted for almost an hour, but they won a victory.

The captain made a careful inspection. The engine-room flooring was charred, and so was a section of the deck; but no serious damage had been done. He was thankful that the gasoline had been emptied from the leaky barrel before the fire broke out. Otherwise they would certainly have been consumed, he thought to himself. But the men, who were thinking the same thing, once again called him "lucky."

"Not lucky," Amundsen said. "There is no such thing. I took precautions when the gasoline was leaking and that saved us, and nothing else."

The following day one of the most vicious storms in Amundsen's experience broke out. It lasted for four nightmarish days. At one moment it seemed as though the doughty little ship which had suffered so many close calls would meet its end. No matter how carefully the captain maneuvered in fighting the wind and the waves, the ship was steadily being driven onto the cruel, jagged coastline of Boothia.

Amundsen turned the ship until its prow pointed at a bit of sandy beach he could dimly make out in the gale—and resolved to drive her up on land at full speed if necessary. But that would be a last resort. Meantime he held fast to the tiller, turning the ship first one way and then the other. As he shouted his defiance, he kept battling the strong currents and the wind. And after four days the *Gjoa,* in practically the same position as when the storm broke, was safe again! It was a superb example of seamanship and, this time, the men did not use the word "luck."

Instead they gathered about him and shook his hand. "You must get some rest," they urged.

"No one gives orders here," he said tiredly. But he let himself be led below, where he fell asleep in a twinkling. He slept for twenty-four hours and awakened ravenously hungry. He ate steadily for almost an hour and then slept for another eight hours. When he came on deck, he was his old self again. The men began to call him the "Viking."

The ship was soon off the coast of King William Island and the captain began to think of winter quarters, for the long Arctic night was in the offing. In Rae Strait they chanced upon a tailor-made shelter. There was a small landlocked bay and all about were great ridges that would keep out the cruel winds.

They hove to at the tiny island and began to move stores from the ship to the land. True scientist that he was, Amundsen took care to see that the delicate instruments were properly established on the island before he gave thought to human shelter. The purposes of the expedition came first, then the men. The crew grumbled, but Amundsen had his way.

First, sites for the instruments were selected. Amundsen paced the island until he found solid, flat rock to use as foundations so as to obvert even the slightest tremor which might cause the instruments to give faulty readings. On top of these foundations he had huge slabs of marble placed, and finally the instruments were set in position. Around the foundations the men dug holes to drain off the water that would form during the spring thaw.

The instruments had been purchased in Germany, which was then the foremost nation of the world in the production of precision measuring devices. They were run by a shrewd clocklike contrivance, and a tiny beam of light told a story on film that patiently revolved past it. Because of the beam it was necessary to enclose the instruments in a dark room. This was constructed of wood from the crates, and the chinks were carefully filed in with bits of cloth until the gloom was Stygian.

It is a fascinating sidelight on the man that he made a note in his diary reminding himself to take along black paper on his future voyages. This consummate passion for preparation and for learning by experience was to prove invaluable in later years, for when planning other trips he never once forgot the rolls of black paper.

The explorer's next thought was for the dogs—not for himself or the men. They constructed several kennel-like houses and saw to it that the beasts were fed and contented before they went on to build shelter for themselves. This forethought for the dogs, which Amundsen knew was a cardinal principle of all polar explorers, made the men grumble once again. But he said simply, "They may save your lives. They must come first."

When all was snug, the men went hunting for fresh meat to lay in store against the winter. In a few days they packed more than one hundred caribou in the ice. The men relished the succulent steaks. They had been without fresh meat for months. The caribou were easy to bring down. The butchering, however, was not a simple affair, for the flesh quickly froze and preparing it was like hacking through stone.

From his reading Amundsen knew how important the livers were and ordered his men to eat a good supply. The Eskimos eagerly ate liver, he had read, and there must be a good reason for it. It wasn't until the 1920s that medical researchists discovered that liver contains great quantities of Vitamin D—an invaluable substitute for sunshine, which is lacking in the Arctic for a good period of the year.

They settled down as comfortably as possible against the long, frozen, dark Arctic night. They had brought along books and simple games. Mornings, Amundsen made them tramp several miles surveying the island and to find more meat even though they had no immediate need. He knew the depression that settles on men during the long, dark siege and he knew, too, that only activity could lift up their spirits. Whenever he saw signs of moodiness or discord, he found work for the men.

So for several months they outwaited the darkness, far in the Arctic wilderness where no man had visited before them.

CHAPTER VI

At Home in an Igloo

The cold set in and bit deeply. The world all about them was held in a viselike grip. As the cold grew more intense, the men left the huts for the snugger bunks aboard ship. But here, as well, the wind sifted in and the discomfort was great. The men were set to packing the exterior of the ship with snow. This quickly froze. On top of the embankment they piled still more snow until the *Gjoa* was wrapped in a great, frozen coat. The vicious, howling winds no longer seeped through the cracks in the planking and for a time, at least, the men had a small measure of comfort.

The dogs took shelter on board, too, though they could have dug themselves into the snow and warmed their dugouts with their own body heat. But they preferred the company of the men aboard, and Amundsen liked to have them around because they provided amusement for the crew.

One morning in November, Amundsen thought he saw caribou off in the distance. He sent the men for their rifles, but as the dark figures, outlined against the ice wastes, drew nearer he wondered. Caribou were fairly stupid, but they did keep their noses in the wind and as a rule did not approach hunters.

The figures continued to advance and he saw they were two-legged. Eskimos! Amundsen put aside his own rifle and ordered two of the armed men to follow him.

As the two parties drew nearer to each other, Amundsen saw that the Eskimos had drawn their bows with arrows and were aiming them at him and his party. He told his men to drop their rifles and to stay where they were while he walked ahead. His heart was pounding, not with fear but with excitement. He threw his arms wide to show that he carried no weapons. Then he stood still and waited for the Eskimos to advance.

The leader of the Eskimos also stopped. After a brief pause for consultation, he threw his bow and arrow aside. The rest of the Eskimos followed suit. Then the two parties continued walking toward each other. There was a solemnity about them that gave way to sudden laughter when one of the Eskimos pointed to Amundsen's face. He appeared to be intrigued by the beard.

The Eskimos, whose tribes are scattered all across the vast Arctic and sub-Arctic regions, number only about thirty thousand. Their Mongoloid features point to Asiatic origin and their faces are practically hairless. That is why the Eskimo enjoyed the sight of Amundsen's spade beard, which looked ludicrous to him.

The captain was quick to recognize the interest and pointed to his own face and broke into laughter. Soon there was laughter all around as the two groups gathered and gestured widely with their hands.

The talk was animated although it consisted solely of grunts, hand waving, and pointing to parts of the body and in general directions. While there are many Eskimo tribes, the language is highly uniform. Very little of it had been set down by Arctic explorers and Amundsen, with all his researches into life in the North, had had no opportunity to master it. Thus neither he nor his men could speak a single word. But they found that there were no barriers to communication.

As Amundsen wrote: "In the primitive parts of the world, language presents no difficulties at all when natives are encountered. These natives have a simple life. Thus they express themselves simply in terms of basic challenges. There are no subtle complexities. Their conversations have to do with the basics of food and shelter, living and dying, birth and pain, joy and sorrow, the full belly or the lean belly, the savage animal or the friendly animal.

"When we encountered this primitive tribe of Eskimos we were concerned with the very same things they were concerned with. Through the use of sign language and a common understanding, we were able to talk to them and they were able to talk to us. All this was done through the medium of common wants. We wanted food and shelter. We feared the hazards of the ice; so did they. It was easy to talk to people with the same problems, hazards and challenges."

Amundsen and his party were the first white men the tribe had even seen. After the preliminaries of mutual understanding were completed by the use of gestures and grunts, he realized that they were trying to tell him that some seventy years ago their grandparents had contact with white men many miles to the east.

The Eskimos indicated the number of years by putting their hands across their eyes to indicate darkness and then suddenly shouting with joy and glancing at the sun. It was tedious but rewarding. When the hands were across the eyes, that meant the season of darkness. When the hands came away from the eyes and they looked up at the sun, that meant the period of light. The whole indicated one year.

Next the leader arranged seven piles of snow. Before each, he squatted and counted on his fingers. Amundsen was puzzled; but when the Eskimo became even more dramatic, he began to understand. The Eskimo smote one of the his men on the head and made him lie down. Then he made a second man kneel alongside the first. Finally he himself stood alongside the pair and with his hand indicated that the trio formed a staircase. "Three generations," Amundsen shouted. "That's what he means."

So, to show that he understood, Amundsen imitated a baby, by crouching down on the snow; then a father, by spanking himself; finally a grandfather, by stooping and hobbling as though he were old and tired.

The Eskimo nodded with delight. Then he went back to the snow piles and counted on his fingers before each pile. There were seven piles and that meant seventy years. Amundsen, recalling his reading, knew he was referring to Sir James Clark Ross, the great Scotch explorer, who had arrived about seventy years ago at a place some twenty-five miles to the east. Later, checking in his small library on board, he found his estimate to be accurate. Sir James, who had died in 1862, was the nephew of Sir John Ross, who had sought the Northwest Passage and later gone to Antarctica.

During the two years the crew of the *Gjoa* lived on the island they got along very well with the Eskimos. Amundsen showed them his marvelous scientific instruments and gave them many presents of tinned food, biscuits, beads and other cheap trinkets he had brought with him.

In return he was able to collect, for museums back home, specimens of every aspect of Eskimo culture. These included weapons, sleds, cooking implements, and wonderful clothing made of caribou skin with black and white designs worked into the shirts and undergarments. The samples of their bead-work, made of caribou teeth and bones, were masterpieces of design. Their entire way of life and, indeed, their survival— their food, shelter, and clothing—depended upon the caribou. What they were able to do with the bones of the caribou was astonishing. By using crude forms they could twist or beat the bones into every imaginable shape. Out of these they made needles, spearheads, arrow tips, and wondrous, beautiful toys for their children.

Frequently the Eskimos had the crew over for dinner, and the men returned their hospitality. Always there was an ex-change of gifts. In return for steel knives, the Eskimos lavished on them exquisite fox pelts which were so perfect that Nor-wegian museums still have them on exhibit today.

There was never any trouble at all. The Norwegians, far from home, showed a tenderness for the Eskimo children that was appreciated by the tribe. When any one of them saw a mem-ber of the crew playing with a child or pelting him with snow, their delight knew no bounds—simply because their children were their proudest possessions. To show their appreciation they ran to the man shouting "Kabluna, kabluna"—the word for white man—and childishly offered themselves as targets for the snowballs.

Amundsen was aware of their poignant gratitude. He was

anxious to study their way of life and become close to them. One day he lectured his men on the need for kindness.

"We are at the mercy of these people. They can wipe us out whenever they wish. They are primitive, but they are not savage. We must be kind. We must be kind to them, to their wives and to their children. We can have a fascinating and instructive time here if we obey the rules of the guest. I know all of us will try."

Soon he took up life with the Eskimos. He went to live in their igloos and joined in their talk; their hunting, fishing, and social problems. He even began to wear Eskimo outfits and he found them to be comfortable and sensible.

"After all," he said, "these people have far more experience up here than I have."

For the two years they remained at the station he tried his best to live the life of the Eskimo, except for his responsibilities to his men and the ship. But to all purposes he dressed, ate, slept, and even tried to think like his new friends. At times the crew thought he was going "native" and chided him or quarreled with him. But he maintained discipline with an iron hand while he continued his life among the primitives. And he learned to communicate in their language.

Frequently Amundsen questioned the Eskimos about the Northwest Passage. They spoke of a clear passage that ran from the east to the west, but he could not determine whether they meant that it extended all the way to the Pacific Ocean. He thought it likely that they referred to a stretch of open water that permitted them to skim along for great distances in their caribou kayaks.

One of the first things he discovered about them was that they had a simple attitude toward time. An hour, a day, a week—these meant nothing at all to them. They understood the two major seasons—the period of light and the period of darkness—and a year. They also understood the idea of a generation and were aware that its span was about twenty-five years. But short periods of time had no importance.

For example, when they took side trips in search of caribou they would just wave to their wives or simply go off without a farewell. Nor would they say how long their trip might take—whether they would return in a day, a week, or a month. While they loved their families, they made little attempt to provide the igloos with food.

They treated themselves with the same indifference. If there was food, they ate. If not, they could travel for days without sustenance and never show irritation, exhaustion, or anxiety. Amundsen smiled recalling how in his youth he had starved himself to prepare for this rigorous existence.

He made copious notes about life in the igloo. He was interested not only in the way they ate, slept, and dressed but also in their psychology, for it seemed to him that, during the two years, he never saw an unhappy Eskimo.

"A hungry Eskimo never looked unhappy. An ill Eskimo never looked unhappy. A tired Eskimo never looked unhappy," he wrote. He questioned Teraiu, an ancient of the tribe, about this. After Amundsen had gone through the motions of crying and laughing, Teraiu understood.

The old man—he was only about thirty-five—grinned and, lying down on the floor, closed his eyes. Amundsen still did not understand. So the leader went out into the snow, scooped a hollow and lay down in it, covered himself with snow and closed his eyes. Amundsen now understood. "There is plenty of time for unhappiness once you're dead," he said, and closed his eyes. Teraiu nodded brightly.

The Eskimos lived well, he found. Though their short life expectancy was due to a badly balanced diet, there were periods during the year when they could harvest almost unlimited quantities of cranberries, a species of wild strawberry, and even dandelions. They ate the wild flowers which grew two feet high in muddy areas and presented gorgeous carpets leading to the great snowy hills and the sheets of icy water. When Amundsen returned to civilization with dried specimens of the vegetation, several learned societies hooted at him and called him a liar. They had the false impression—one that earlier explorers had not troubled to correct—that the so-called Frigid Zone was a place of constant, sustained, frozen-over wastes.

He also found that, while the caribou was the mainstay of their culture, at certain times of the year they enjoyed ducks, geese, a huge species of swan, plovers, hardy sparrows, gulls, gigantic owls (almost all of which were albinos), mice, and tern. These they killed with their arrows or by means of clever traps made of mosses. From the hundreds of thousands of migratory birds that came to nest, they had a fantastic supply of eggs which they sucked raw. There were, as well, Arctic hares, the bear, the lemming, and the fox.

The architecture of the igloo was not, as commonly supposed, a matter of one icy brick laid upon another. What the Eskimos did, to afford greater strength and wind resistance, was to lay the ice blocks round and round and round in spiral fashion which ever narrowed to the top. Later, in talking to architects in Europe, Amundsen was told that the spiral method of constructing a cone-shaped house allowed the utmost resistance to stresses and strains.

"Chances are," the architects told him, "that the original Eskimos brought this method from the Asiatic continent from which they came perhaps thousands of years ago. In Tibet, for example, and in other northerly Asiatic regions, a hut made of mud blocks, laid spirally, is a common sight. Your Eskimos probably did not even know that the building plan had come from their ancestors."

And it was true that they had no sense of history or origin except for amusing tales that had come from no one more remote than perhaps a great-grandfather. Teraiu was a great one for spelling out wondrous tales of his grandfather, who presumably was a great hunter.

The anecdote of his grandfather's conquest of two bears at one time, no matter how frequently told, always brought applause and great merriment from the tribe. It seemed that the great hunter deliberately stood between a mother bear and a father bear while clutching a cub.

Both great beasts rushed at him at the same time. He neatly side-stepped and let them slip and slide into each other, cracking their heads and stunning themselves. "It was an easy matter," Teraiu related graphically, illustrating with two children, "for Grandfather to knock both of them on the head with his club and then stab them in their throats."

Amundsen won the tribal leader's undying affection by scribbling on paper as though he were taking down the account of this exploit with the greatest care. "Teraiu," he wrote, "behaved exactly like a vain explorer when he is being interviewed by a reporter for *The New York Times*." The old man loved the attention and it was this, and his courtesy, that allowed

Amundsen to take up his place in igloo life without much difficulty.

The Eskimos were curious about his body, for they wanted to see whether he was made the way they were. He was forced to strip naked, despite his embarrassment, and allow the men and women to inspect him, poke him, and make comments about him. All this was done gravely. The men were especially entranced with the slight hair on his chest and one of them wondered whether he was related to the bear.

The old leader, who was not without humor, told Amundsen that the tribe wanted to hunt him. "You are like a bear," he said, chuckling.

"I really believe they are making a far more intensive study of my body, my customs, my way of living than I'm making of theirs," he told the crew. "They have a healthy curiosity, but it's almost impossible to describe to them life in our civilization."

On one of his lecture tours in later years, he made a point of stressing the fact that, while the Eskimo is not afforded the shelter and comfort of civilized life, "he yet has a more leisurely, philosophical and sensible life than we have. The Eskimo does not rush about to make a living; he does not have to dress to conform to style, only to the climate; he does not have to be polite except as his own good nature makes him amiable; he does not have to dance attendance on a boss or his work; and he thoroughly enjoys life because he gives himself over to the love of his family, to outdoor sports, to sleeping and to eating—when he has food."

The interiors of the igloos were foul-smelling. They were rank with decayed food; with the oil, extracted from animals, which they used for lighting; with unwashed bodies; with dogs.

Their feasts consisted of raw sides of caribou and melted snow. These were set on a pile of moss in the center of the lodgings and everyone pulled out a knife, grabbed a chunk and went to work on it. Rarely was any great section of meat left in the center of the floor, no matter how few the diners.

During mealtime there was great talk. Gigantic lies, not without humor, were told. Everyone chuckled, ate ravenously, pressed food into Amundsen's lap, shouted at the children, and sweated in the close atmosphere. Once the banquet was over, there were no "brandies and coffee," as Amundsen put it, but everyone took off all his clothing and went to sleep. There were no guest bedrooms.

Amundsen shrugged, took off his own clothing, and went to sleep in the mass of naked bodies. "Sometimes the interests of science and research make for an embarrassing life," he wrote. "I don't think I ever blushed so much as when I undressed in my first igloo with two families looking on curiously."

Amundsen noted there was very little petty larceny. All property appeared to be community-owned—a way of life that is common among most aboriginal tribes, which face hardship and danger and cling together for the common good and for safety. "A man who worked hard on a pair of snowshoes might call them his own. But he did not think of it that way, exactly," Amundsen explained. "In other words, if he left them outdoors, another member of the tribe could borrow them and go off with them for days on end without inviting recriminations or anger."

Nor did the Eskimos have a sense of private ownership of their wives. They loved them and had children by them, but their principles of morality differed from those of the Western world. The family feeling was deep and abiding, but the sense of belonging to a tribe and "sharing" was perhaps more important. "Because of this," Amundsen wrote, "I had an understanding why these kind people were never lonely as we know loneliness and aloneness in the big cities of the world."

The dogs were a part of the family but also part of the community property. The Eskimos frequently fed their dogs before they themselves dined. But they were sparing with food for the animals when there was not enough to go around among all.

The human factor, Amundsen wrote, came first and foremost. "My guess is that children would be allowed to die during a period of want rather than the elders." And he told about the time he went fishing with several of the tribe, including a father and his young son.

When a kayak overturned in a swift-rushing current, "everyone rushed to save the father. They swam out, put out their own boats, went leaping from ice floe to ice floe holding out long spears—all to the father, who was clutching the edge of the kayak. The boy went spinning off into the distance and was soon lost to sight forever."

While he was shocked at this, he tried to understand. "In our world, the child is always saved. But in the world of the North, it is the adult who is important to the tribe and to the family. He is the one who can hunt and fish and provide shelter and comfort. He is more important than his offspring."

There was crying after the loss and death of the child, but it was of short duration. "Not because they are unfeeling people," Amundsen said. "But because they must be realistic. The father of the family is the fountainhead of food and shelter and they just don't know sentimentality about children.

It's a simple matter of arithmetic. The greater the number of adults in the tribe, the better the security. The larger the number of children, the greater the number of dependents and, hence, the lesser the security."

Within a space of hours the death of the child and the rescue of the father were both forgotten. It was a commonplace occurrence in the life of the tribe. Several studies have been made of the religious sensibility of the Eskimo and his primitive concept of a god or gods. Amundsen's theory was that they had a paganlike attitude toward sun, darkness, animals, danger, taboos, which made for a loose and indecisive religious feeling. He did not encounter what may be termed a religious leader, witch doctor, or code of morals based upon religion.

One day Amundsen asked the tribal chief whether a party would accompany him on a trek that might take several months. It was his intention to head in the general direction of what he was sure would be the site of the Magnetic Pole. The tribe was only too happy to accommodate their new friend who had such an interest in their affairs. That night they gave what might be called a dance. It was held in a huge igloo which served as a kind of meeting place.

The crew was invited and sat fascinated watching the somewhat cumbersome and heavy steps of the squat Eskimo women, who danced by themselves or in groups. The moss wicks floating in basins of oil lighted up the room and threw fantastic shadows as the women cavorted in their soft shoes. The men hummed a monotonous chant to the accompaniment of a huge, rude drum beaten by one of the Eskimos.

The drum was fashioned from several rib bones of a caribou.

Across the top a caribou skin had been stretched taut and was held in place by thongs made of caribou sinews.

One of the women seized a member of the crew, lifted him to his feet from his crouching position, and whirled him round and round. The Eskimos roared and cheered, and soon everyone was dancing while the drummer kept up his endless thumping. The hilarity lasted until dawn.

A great feast of raw meat was set out and the Eskimos set to. The Europeans were famished but too exhausted to eat. There was merriment as one woman approached Amundsen and shoved a big chunk of meat into his mouth. He rose, bowed gallantly, and then tottered. Everyone laughed. But he followed the example of the rest and ate, though all he wanted to do was sleep.

Before the sun was very high, the small party of six was on its way. They did not stop for food all that day. Amundsen was glad he had been gallant and eaten what the woman had proffered him.

He was gone from base for more than three months, but his Eskimo friends attended him carefully all the while. The trek was an endless nightmare of snowy wastes. For days on end they starved. Amundsen had a compass with him, and several instruments mounted on sleds. He took observations whenever he could manage to shake himself out of his lethargy and exhaustion. Whenever he pointed, the Eskimos cheerfully nodded and hurried forward. Never did they take a short cut around a rise in the ground. When he leveled his finger after taking a sight, they plunged right on and took him with them. They wanted to show their devotion.

During this nightmarish trip he passed directly over the exact spot where the Magnetic Pole has since been located.

But he never knew it. For one thing, he could not keep up with the Eskimos. For another, his instruments became almost chaotic as he drew nearer and nearer the shifting Magnetic Pole. They registered all kinds of influences simply because they were not so exact or so attuned to the magnetic disturbances as are today's instruments, which can compensate for the more powerful magnetisms in action about the Magnetic Pole.

En route the Eskimos amused themselves by playing a simple football game. They blew up a caribou-skin ball and kicked it about until everyone dropped on the ice from sheer exhaustion. There were no rules, no scoring. Everyone just kicked and scampered and ran up and down the rolling ice plains.

Amundsen joined them occasionally and became a kind of champion because he knew enough to kick the ball to one side when another player deployed to get it away from him. Then he turned sharply and kicked it the other way. When still another player came running up, he swiveled and kicked it slightly in a different direction and seized control by swiveling again. His soccer games in Norway stood him in good stead. The Eskimos were entranced. They had only known about kicking one way to another player, who would kick back to them. Amundsen gave them a new perspective on the game and they practiced skirmishing, weaving, and faking passes with their feet until they all dropped on the ice with merriment over the new developments introduced into their ancient game.

The moment that excited them most was when Amundsen got underneath the soaring ball and butted it with his head. The whole group then flopped over backwards on the ice, kicked upwards, as Amundsen put it, "like so many huge, furry insects happy over the anointing of a queen."

When he returned to base, lean, haggard, and full of tales, the crew stared at him as though he had returned from the dead. They had given him up for lost.

"No Magnetic Pole, as far as I know," he said. "I just can't tell. But I know I wasn't far off."

The crew, dispirited by his long absence, had several times been about to set sail without him. But always the ancient leader, Teraiu, intervened. "He kept pointing to the North and smiling," one of the crew said. "He was sure that the Eskimos with you would return. Some of them anyhow. But he was never quite sure you would be with the party."

Amundsen grinned through cracked, blackened lips. "I wasn't too sure myself. These boys set a rugged pace. They're the best explorers in history. If only they could write and draw maps! I could then stay home and read about it."

It was time to close camp and say good-bye—a sad day for everyone. There was no kissing, for this gesture is not an Eskimo custom. Instead, when all were gathered about on the shore, they hugged one another and rubbed noses.

There were tears in the eyes of Amundsen and many of the crew as they set sail. It was like leaving an ancient civilization they were never to see again. The Eskimos, as well, were astonishingly emotional. They brought gifts to the ship, held up their children for a final farewell, waved and waved, and literally danced on the snow.

From afar the white man heard the sad, mournful pounding of the huge drum which had been dragged up to the shore. "We will miss those good, cheerful friends. I don't think we'll ever meet better people in our lifetime," the captain said.

CHAPTER VII

Through the Zigzag Atop the World

The *Gjoa* now headed west in search of the Northwest Passage. The splendid library which Amundsen had purchased from an old man in England was a guiding finger. He was able, by close study, to divorce the poor surmises of the earlier explorers from the good guesses and to fashion his own ideas. Thus he benefited from the mistakes of those who had gone before him.

The multitude of maps crudely drawn by pioneers, and their loose accounts, seemed to indicate that the most likely route lay west from the northern sector of Boothia Felix. However, this route, Amundsen saw, was a trap into which earlier explorers had fallen. By correlating one account with the next, he noted that one adventurer after the other had attempted the route only to meet with impassable ice or land masses. He resolved not to go over the same ground or up against the same barriers. He sought a navigable water route and that alone—not a water and land route. Sir Leopold's account of the Franklin Expedition gave him the clue he needed. He staked the course of the *Gjoa* on a path far south of any undertaken previously.

It was on August 13, 1905, that they broke camp and headed for Simpson Strait. The coastline had been charted by overland explorers, but no one had attempted to cover the region by ship. On and on they crawled, using just a minimum of sail and taking soundings every twenty-five feet.

It was a rugged and heartbreaking trip, for each moment appeared to be their last as the ship's keel kept scraping on the jagged, rocky bottom. The days were wearisome, for the negotiation of the channels was an ever-winding, labyrinthine affair. At times a channel was so narrow and curving that the small *Gjoa* had difficulty snaking and turning to get into a basin farther along. But a steady hand at the tiller kept the historic ship edging its way across the top of the world from east to west.

At several points in Simpson Strait, soundings indicated that there was just an inch of water between the keel and the bottom. The grinding and scraping shook the ship from stem to stern.

This slow, tortuous voyage lasted for three dismal weeks. A sudden storm, a great boulder in their path, an unsteady hand at the tiller, or a slackening in taking soundings would have meant an end to the ship and the crew.

Amundsen was beside himself as day followed day in slow procession. He knew he was going in a westerly direction; but how long he could go that way, he could not judge. He could not eat or sleep. His eyes were red-rimmed; his face grew gaunt and his skin yellowed. The men begged him to turn back, but he refused. "We'll get through, I think," he said. "When we can't go any farther, we'll turn back. That's all there is to it."

So they went on, winding, twisting, turning, crawling. Sometimes they headed back east, when the channels curved back on themselves in hairpin turns. Sometimes they turned north and then abruptly south. At times they went east for miles and miles, swung about when there was an opening, and turned west again.

One night they hove to while the captain napped for an hour. The crew had a conference which was broken up when Amundsen suddenly appeared on deck. He was unshaven and his eyes were terrible to look at, but he held himself in check.

"Miserable men!" he shouted. "What are you up to? What do you want? Why did you come on this voyage?" He glared about and then laughed. "Now look," he said, "we have been together for a long time. We have plenty of food aboard that our Eskimo friends gave up. The ship is behaving well. We are all healthy. What's this little exploration? Nothing! Let's go on until we're stopped."

They crawled; they swiveled back on themselves; they ran into soft ice and plowed through. But on and on they went.

At night they burned flares on the deck to help the man at the tiller see his way. Once when they were sailing in a northerly direction it got so cold that one of the crew said they would soon touch the shores of Siberia. "We've gone over the North Pole," the man said. "We're back in the Eastern Hemisphere."

"Good," Amundsen said. "Maybe we can claim a new record. That means we'll soon be dining with the Czar in Moscow. Just a little while longer and we'll be the first to have sailed across the top of the world from the Western Hemisphere to the Eastern. The *Gjoa* will go down in history as a ferryboat. And each of us will be the greatest ferryboatman the world has ever known."

In two weeks they passed schools of fish—big fish that leaped and cavorted. They were in a great basin. Amundsen stared with delight. This, to him, was a sign that they were nearing open water. He dropped a line and with the help of two men hauled up a gigantic salmon. "Impossible!" he cried.

They roasted the huge fish and devoured it. Then there were five days when ice and snowbanks and close shores again turned the Passage into a creepy, crawling channel.

"Sounding!" shouted Amundsen. "Sounding!" echoed the leadman. And so it went, for nights and days, until once again they were in the open with nothing ahead of them but the horizon. But again the shores grew nearer and once more the *Gjoa* limped onward with little sail or none at all. Sometimes they used the auxiliary engine to creep along so that they would not be at the mercy of the slightest breeze.

One morning there was a strong gale. It carried with it a salty tang that was unfamiliar. They had for long been in the Arctic, which percolated only fresh and icy winds. But here it was different. This was an ocean scent, spicy and sharp. Too, they detected an indefinable softness along with the salt.

Amundsen climbed the mast. The men watched him eagerly. He lifted his nose to the wind, sniffed, and clambered down. "Two more days," he said with aplomb. "Just two more days." Later he confessed that he only tossed off a time limit in order to hearten the men. "How could I judge where the Pacific was and how soon, if ever, we could reach it? I could smell it. But smells drift thousands of miles. I had hope, but nothing more."

Two days later, at dawn, he was seized with a racking cough. He could barely manage to hold the tiller, but he waved away efforts to relieve him. "This is my day," he croaked. "I'll take her through the last hours." And he steered on and on. It was August 26. He had not eaten for days. He was ill and spent. But the men looked at the calendar and trusted to the captain. He had said two days and two days it should be.

He stood at the tiller and relied on his reputation for luck. If it held, he would be fine. If it did not, he would be ashamed to face his men. Once again he smelled the salt breeze and felt invigorated. It was impossible that they were not close. Impossible!

By noon he could see open water ahead. A swell of joy went through him. He felt sure he had won through.

At nightfall he was still at the tiller, faint, weak, and dizzy. He saw a white triangle ahead, but he thought it was a dancing mirage of his own imaging. Then from on high, from the lookout, there came a cry: "Sail! Sail ahead! A sail! A sail! A sail ahead! A sail! Sail ho! Sail ho!"

Amundsen burst into tears. He knew instantly what he had achieved. It was a sail. And it belonged to the *Charles Hansson,* out of San Francisco on the west coast of the United States, beating its way to the north.

He turned the tiller over to one of the men. The crew burst into tears. No one was ashamed to cry.

Roald Amundsen had negotiated the Northwest Passage— the first man in history to navigate the top of the world from ocean to ocean.

He went from man to man and smacked each on the cheek. "Why are you crying?" he asked, crying himself. "You didn't think we could do it?" he demanded to know. The crew looked at him and he looked at them, while the *Charles Hansson* heeled to starboard.

Amundsen was seized by an emotion such as he never again experienced. He did a dance on the deck. He abandoned dignity. He kissed the crew again on both cheeks. His mood passed to his crew. The men began to caper and dance.

Later, when they talked about it, they were ashamed. But it was a momentary release from the strain and the high tensions. They had done what no other men had ever done. They had negotiated the Northwest Passage and they celebrated it as perhaps Columbus and his crew had marked the landing on the shore of the New World, or as Marco Polo had when he and his caravan arrived in fabled Cathay in the Far East.

Amundsen was suddenly relaxed. The pent-up feelings of the arduous weeks had left him. A violent hunger seized him. Knife in hand, he ran up the rigging into the shrouds where a carcass of caribou was hanging.

He steadied himself with one arm and with the other he slashed at the meat and, hacking off slices, he ate and ate the raw chunks like a savage. It felt good. Then, still hanging on the spidery ladder in the shrouds, he became violently nauseous. When he felt better he cut more slices off the caribou meat, went down the ladder with them, and ate with dignity. This time he was able to keep them down. The crew respected his emotion and abandon. After his keen appetite was satiated, he felt warmed and contented. Then he went to sleep. It was the first good sleep he had had in three weeks.

The terrible weeks had taken a toll. Though he was only thirty-three when he negotiated the Passage, he looked sixty-six. He was to remain aged-looking for the rest of his life, old before his time; lean, gaunt, and severe-looking, though inside of himself he had real warmth and understanding.

They were now en route to the Bering Sea, which Amundsen was sure would allow them clear sailing. On September 2, as they hove to off King Point on the northern coast of Canada, winter came in with an unseasonable rush and the big freeze was on as the Arctic night descended.

There was no going on as the ice thickened and spread. The crew could almost watch it drawing nearer. Amundsen decided to freeze in at King Point. Nearby, at Herschel Island, were several whaling vessels, also frozen in.

Amundsen was wild with impatience to let the world know about his triumph. The sailors aboard the whalers were not impressed with his story when he paid them a visit. Nor were their captains. Their indifference did not deflate him because he knew they were rough, hard-working men who did not recognize the importance of negotiating the long-sought Passage. He was sure the world would hail him and was feverish to get to a telegraph office to flash the news. But it was to be a long time before he could do so.

He had now been gone for more than two years. Though he had never had much contact with his brothers, who led a completely different kind of life, he still felt a pang for home, friends, and family. He often wondered whether anyone missed him. He also wondered whether the *Gjoa,* because it had sailed away under a cloud of debt, was listed as "lost" by the maritime insurance firm of Lloyds of London, which kept track of ships at sea.

He wondered, too, whether the world would care very much that he had negotiated the Northwest Passage. He knew that most persons were completely unaware of the search for the

Passage and would be indifferent to its discovery. But would the fact that so many lives had been lost in earlier attempts count for anything, make any impression?

These thoughts he kept to himself because essentially, like all leaders of exploration, he was a lonely man. He knew, for example, that his crew, while elated, was not especially overcome with the conquest of the Passage. Nor were the members intrigued by his notes on the social life of the Eskimo. They looked upon his interest in the Eskimo as an unimportant, intellectual hobby. They could not recognize the valuable contributions he had made to the study of aboriginal man, nor that what he had found would be described in geography textbooks throughout the world.

One of the new friends he made in port was a Captain Phineas Mogg of the whaler *Bonanza*. Mogg was anxious to make an attempt to reach San Francisco by an overland route so that he could command another whaling vessel without losing almost a year frozen in the ice. He was willing to finance Amundsen, who was penniless, if he would make the trip with him. Amundsen did not especially like the man, but he consented because of his own anxiety to get to civilization and flash the news. He realized that Captain Mogg, because he had the money, would insist upon heading the overland trek, but he did not care.

The whaling captain provisioned the dog sleds with frozen beans instead of the pemmican Amundsen preferred for a trip in the frozen North. But Mogg had his way. Amundsen was often to think of the lovely tins of dried meat and fat on his *Gjoa* as they made their way overland accompanied by an Eskimo, Jim, and his wife, Kappa.

The foursome used a dozen dogs and two sleds. Amundsen

was in poor condition because of the arduous weeks in the narrow channels when he had gone without sleep and food. However, a few days on the trail hardened him. Soon he was his old self again and working along with Jim to break the snow in front of the dogs.

The whaling captain, who was short and plump, refused to do his share and persisted in riding atop the heavy sacks of beans on one of the sleds. He was giving the dogs a bad time and refused to take his turn at breaking the trail.

"I put up the money and I'm a passenger," he said smugly.

"No one is a passenger on a trip like this, Captain," Amundsen said. "We all share in the work."

"You are wrong, my friend," the fat captain said. "You are very wrong."

In a little while Mogg was complaining about the food. "I'm hungry. I'm starving to death. These beans aren't enough. I thought you experienced travelers planned better," he said.

Amundsen looked at him incredulously. "I urged that we take along pemmican. Don't you remember?"

"I don't remember. You planned this trip," Mogg said. "I'm starving and I'm going to faint." He fell off the sled and refused to budge.

Jim grinned at Amundsen. "Let's eat him before the wolves get him," the Eskimo said. "He has lots of good fat on him."

"That's a wonderful idea," Amundsen said.

Both men advanced on him, champing their teeth fiendishly and snarling. Mogg, horrified, rose with alacrity and clambered atop the sacks of beans, and for several days he uttered not a word of complaint.

Then he forgot his terror and again complained about the steady diet of beans. Jim merely turned to the dogs and in thick guttural tones started to sic them on the frightened man. At the same time he and Amundsen advanced on Mogg.

"In the North a man eats when he is hungry," Amundsen said. "He eats anything. I am hungry for fat. I will eat you." He grabbed the captain and flung him on the ground. The captain began to cry and the explorer felt sorry. "Just keep quiet and everything will be all right," he said. "We're all hungry because you insisted that we take along nothing but beans. A man needs fats in this part of the country, and the pemmican would have been perfect. You had better keep quiet because I'm as hungry as you are."

In a few weeks they surmounted the nine thousand feet of peaks and soon began to drop down to the Yukon River where there was a fort and a trading post. Nights, they shivered and starved because, as Amundsen said, the beans did not give them the nutritional body heat they required. There was a definite hostility between the two of them which Amundsen decided to keep at a low pitch simply because Mogg was inexperienced.

At Fort Yukon the two Eskimos were left behind and Amundsen and Captain Mogg continued on alone to make the run to civilization. Mogg still persisted in riding the sled, with Amundsen breaking the path ahead. At times Mogg complained that the explorer wasn't going fast enough. An old hand at dealing with people in the wilderness, where there is a vital need for cooperation, Amundsen at one point threatened to leave Mogg and go back on foot to Fort Yukon. This frightened Mogg so much that he agreed to trot alongside the sled and complain no more.

On December 5, 1905, with the temperature standing at

sixty degrees below zero, the pair arrived at Fort Egbert, the northernmost post of the United States Army.

Amundsen was greeted with astonishment by the commander. For one thing, he was not accustomed to visitors who dropped in from the North at this time of the year. For another, here was a visitor—one about whom he had read— claiming to have negotiated the Northwest Passage.

"You are Road Amundsen?" the army man asked in amazement.

"Yes, I am Roald Amundsen," the explorer said with embarrassment. "Why do you ask?"

"Why, I read about you just yesterday in a newspaper three months old that arrived last week," the commander said. And he showed Amundsen the paper.

The story, published in a Chicago paper, said that the *Gjoa* had foundered in an Arctic gale and was presumed lost. A fishing vessel off Greenland had found a floating case with the ship's name on it. Amundsen thought for a moment. This must have been part of the "dark hut" he had erected for the scientific instruments; it must have floated away and been found. Then word of the floating case had reached Europe and the news had been relayed to the United States. In due course the paper in which the story had been printed was sent by rail and steamer to Alaska and arrived at Fort Egbert, where it was read by the commander.

And here, a week later, the man about whom the story had been written showed up at the post! It was incredible.

"Small world," Amundsen said.

"Big man," the commander said, pumping his hand. "I am proud to know you, sir. I know all about the Northwest Passage. This post up here gives me much time to read—especially about the North. I'm sure my children and grandchildren will read about you someday, sir."

The thought had never struck Amundsen. His face crimsoned beneath his Arctic tan. "It was nothing. Just sailing, sir," he said. Then he begged permission to use the army telegraph line which trailed for thousands of miles across Alaska to continental United States. The fort actually was the last post on the telegraph line.

The commander readily agreed. Amundsen filed a thousand words informing the world of his successful passage, and directed the message to Oslo newspapers. Unfortunately his good luck did not hold; for soon after the sergeant began sending the electrifying news, a fierce cold snap parted the line a hundred miles below the fort. It was a whole week later that the story was sent out and congratulations began pouring in to the lonely outpost from all over the world. The army cooperated gallantly in relaying the messages.

Amundsen did not at first realize the extent of the world's reaction. Full realization came later and startled him. That time was to be perhaps the most pleasurable of his life; for while he was a modest man, he enjoyed success and its fruits. He had earned the plaudits of the world.

He left Fort Egbert alone the following February, after a recuperative stay, and made his way north to the *Gjoa*. The trip was almost pleasant without Captain Mogg and his complaints. He picked up Jim and Kappa at Fort Yukon. When they reached Porcupine River they rubbed their eyes in amazement, for there was a lone man trudging along on foot. "Look," said Jim in his halting English. "Look, a man without a dog or a sled."

The man turned out to be Arthur Darrell, a postman, who

delivered mail from the Mackenzie River to trading posts in the wild country. Amundsen considered Darrell the bravest man he had ever known. To travel the frozen North without a friend, a dog, or a sled is a fantastic thing, yet Darrell had been doing it for years. For a long time afterward Amundsen corresponded with this hardy postman and he felt very sad when he received news that Darrell had been lost in a violent snowstorm at the mouth of the Mackenzie.

By July the ice had thawed sufficiently to free the ship. The *Gjoa* then sailed for Point Barrow, made its way through Bering Strait, and set a course for San Francisco.

In his wildest dreams Amundsen never expected what he encountered. When the ship tied up at a small dock and he brought out his clearance papers for the customs official, the man shoved back his hat and said, "You're Amundsen?"

"Yes, sir," the captain replied.

The customs man shook his hand and said, "Wait a moment, please. We've been expecting you." He turned and ran up the pier to an office and dispatched a messenger.

In the space of two hours incredible things began to happen. Meantime the men were anxious to go ashore and have a shave and a haircut and look at the sights. This was to be denied them for many hours.

While they fretted, the customs man asked them to be patient. "I have my orders, sir. You can't land until I get permission. You're going to have a big bust-up."

And bust-up it was. For the rest of the day Amundsen and his bearded men were honored guests of the city. Newspapermen hounded them; photographers took their pictures; public officials shook their hands. They were then ushered to the Palace Hotel, where the finest accommodations were placed at their disposal without charge. The men were thunderstruck.

"The Northwest Passage is important, then?" one of the crew asked him.

"I suppose," Amundsen answered smilingly.

Not long after, several government and learned societies struck off medals which were presented to him by ambassadors and consuls. He received scrolls from other groups, and degrees from universities. He became a public speaker, though at first he was nervous before an audience.

With fame, there came money. His lecture tours, which took him all over the United States and Europe, were triumphant. He told about his experiences in the channels and about his life with the Eskimos. Still he felt uneasy. "I think I'm being a performer," he told a friend.

"You are wrong. People are seriously interested in what you have to tell them," the friend said. "They want to learn about the world they have never seen. You are giving them a lecture in geography and social customs. You are a teacher when you lecture. Don't look down on yourself."

The next time he spoke, he tried to watch the faces of the people in front of him. The audience respected him and listened to him with rapt interest.

"I suppose I'm a great man," he told himself in the mirror. "Anything but that," the mirror spoke back to him. "Anything but that. You haven't done anything yet." He nodded and agreed.

He returned to Norway with money enough to repay his creditors from whom he had fled in the *Gjoa*. They felt honored to have the great man owe them money and many refused to accept his payment, saying, "We wish to have a part in the great voyage. Norway is proud of you and we Norsemen understand the expensive business of exploration. Besides," they added, "we can tell our grandchildren that we helped to finance a great expedition they will read about." And so they clapped him on the back and asked him to dinner. This was a far cry from the night he and his crew lifted sail and stole out of the harbor. It seemed ages ago.

Now it was 1907 and Amundsen had funds with which to start dreaming of a new, high adventure. This time he dreamed of the North Pole. In a new ship. He had presented the *Gjoa* to the city of San Francisco, where with all due ceremony she had been placed in the famous Golden Gate Park hard by the Pacific Ocean—where she could hear the waves she once triumphed over in her historic voyage from the Atlantic to the Pacific through the zigzag atop the world.

CHAPTER VIII

From the Top to the Bottom

The *Fram* was not a lovely ship, but she was broad of beam and stout. She had been built not for beauty but to resist the bear hugs of crushing ice. She took a shallow draft and did not care a bit for speed. To help her along she had a small auxiliary motor.

She had been specially constructed for Dr. Fridtjof Nansen when he got the idea that he could discover the North Pole by drifting across it. Dr. Nansen felt sure there was a drift that would take him from Bering Strait to the Arctic Ocean. His notion was to enter the Strait in the stout *Fram,* get frozen in by the ice, drift, get frozen in again, and then let the Northern waters take him across the top of the world directly over the North Pole.

His expedition failed because his theory of drift did not work out. The *Fram* was frozen in, drifted, was frozen in again, and never came near the Pole at all.

Amundsen felt sure that if he entered Bering Straight at a different time of the year he would find the drift to be different. He was confident that by using Nansen's theory he could win to the Pole.

He found no difficulty in raising funds for his new expedition. Rich men and scientific societies vied with each other in lending him support and supplies. Frequently he discussed with Nansen his own plans for a "drift operation" across the Pole and he tried to learn how and why Nansen's theory had gone awry.

"Why did you fail?" he asked the great man.

"I did not fail," Nansen answered. "My tide and drift theory failed. We went wherever the *Fram* took us. It just didn't take us where we wanted to go." Then he showed on maps of his own making why he thought there was a drift over the Pole. "Perhaps if you entered here"—he indicated Bering Strait— "in the spring of the year, instead of in the fall as I did, you'd be taken over the top."

Amundsen purchased the *Fram*, refitted and reconditioned her, placed stores in her, had the motor tuned up, and set about hiring the kind of men he liked and wanted—men with a dash of adventure, yet hardy and sensible.

Soon he was ready to go. The *Fram* was completely equipped with all the necessaries for the try at the North Pole. He estimated that the adventure would take from two to three years. If only we can get into the right ice pack at the right time, he thought wistfully. The North Pole is surrounded by a floating ice pack, while the South Pole is circled by mountain ranges, glaciers, and land masses which can only be traversed on foot.

There happened then one of the most fantastic exploration reversals in history. It may be likened to the flight made by Douglas Corrigan—"Wrong Way" Corrigan as the newspapers labeled him—who was supposed to fly to the west coast of the United States but landed, instead, in Ireland. "I lost my sense of direction," Corrigan told the press, and won the plaudits of an amused world. Amundsen did the very same thing!

The *Fram* was all set to sail on her drifting expedition to the North Pole when suddenly it was announced that his old friend Dr. Cook, with whom he had sailed on the *Belgica*, had been to the Pole. Cook was on his way to Denmark on a steamer and was to be interviewed by Peter Freuchen, the famous Arctic expert and explorer.

Freuchen finally spoke with Cook and did not quite like the account he gave. There were several discrepancies in Cook's story, Freuchen felt. However, because he was at the time working for a newspaper, Freuchen did not feel he should venture an opinion. Dr. Cook went on to be feted and honored until suddenly a great scandal broke. Cook was called a liar by Admiral Robert Edwin Peary. The United States Admiral cabled to say that he himself had reached the Pole and that any claims put forth by Cook were false and fraudulent.

Meantime Amundsen was disappointed that he had not had a chance to reach the Pole himself. But he gave full credit to anyone who had and he kept an open mind about Cook's claim. One night he was approached by Freuchen in Copenhagen. The two great men spoke all night about Cook's claims. When dawn broke, Amundsen was still reiterating his faith in his old friend Dr. Cook. They resolved to head an expedition to Etah, in northern Greenland, to find two diaries Cook said he had left there. However, it was difficult to raise money for the expedition and, moreover, Cook himself did not like the idea. "I don't need any substantiation. My own word is good enough," he said.

Not long afterward various scientific societies said that

Cook, who had been honored, feted, and given many cash prizes, was a fraud. This decision led to many years of grief and distress for countless persons—including Amundsen, who had much affection for his old friend.

Now that the Pole had been discovered, either by Peary or by Cook, Amundsen's backers grew cold and withdrew their offers of support. And many who had already given him money wanted it returned. "The show is over," they said. "The North Pole has been discovered. We want our money back."

Amundsen was without funds except for the meager sums he had left over from the lecture tours he had made after purchasing the *Fram*. He could no longer hope for new backers. The Pole had been won, the glamour of first discovery was gone, and his onetime supporters were no longer interested.

Here he was with a good ship on his hands, a splendid crew, excellent supplies, and no place to go. Well, I have a place to go, he thought, stroking his long chin.

Blandly he issued an announcement, which ran in the world press, saying he was glad Peary had discovered the North Pole but that he found much scientific worth in trying Nansen's drift method. "We will learn much about Arctic Ocean tides and ice pack drifts that way," he declared.

He also said that he would sail to the Madeira Islands; make his way around Cape Horn and up to Bering Strait, where the *Fram* would be allowed to drift, be frozen in, and then drift again. "We will then achieve the North Pole," he said.

But he had other ideas in mind. He knew he needed no money for the place where he intended to go, for there would be no way to spend it. However he would need more food— to add to the supply he had already placed aboard the *Fram*, months ago. Meanwhile he himself was preparing pemmican in a small bakeshop he had rented. He cooked meat and fat in equal proportions, did his own canning, and stored his entire output aboard the *Fram*. His funds were low, but his spirits were high. He smiled to himself like a small boy. He had a secret he told no one about.

He sang as he worked and his friends who wandered in, to observe how an explorer prepares food for a trip, were astonished. "Peary or Cook, one or the other, has stolen your triumph," they said. "What makes you so happy?"

"I have a secret," Amundsen replied. "I'm going to the North Pole and bring it back to Denmark. That will make Peary or Cook look like a fool. Does that satisfy you?"

The *Fram* reached the Madeira Islands in September of 1910. Amundsen had all hands gathered on deck and then broke the news. "We are supposed to try and reach the North Pole," he said. "But it has been reached, as all of you know. How about trying to reach the South Pole?" And he burst into laughter.

The crew was stunned. Then they broke into cheers. They laughed and cheered and laughed again. Then they picked Amundsen up bodily and paraded with him about the deck. The *Fram* set sail for the Antarctic.

Amundsen had never set foot on the Antarctic Continent proper, despite his early experiences on the *Belgica* when she was frozen in. But he had read and reread the accounts written by several explorers concerning their attempts to gain the South Pole. When the *Fram* left Norway, he was asked several times why he had one hundred Husky dogs in kennels on the deck. He merely said that he like Eskimo dogs.

Newspapermen, who had learned a great deal about the

Arctic since the Peary-Cook imbroglio broke, wondered why he needed Huskies if he was going to drift to the North Pole. "After all," one reporter wrote in his paper, "Mr. Amundsen is not going to swim across the North Pole with one hundred Husky dogs holding him up. He must have other plans we don't know about. Who knows? They may include the moon. But he certainly does not need dogs for his 'drift operation.' "

The crew now knew why the dogs had been brought all the way from Greenland before they sailed. They cheered, the dogs barked, and the *Fram* proceeded south for the Bay of Whales.

Meantime another expedition, the ill-fated Scott group, was on its way to try and reach the South Pole. The discovery of the Pole on top had set into motion various plans for getting to the Pole on the bottom. Peary's glory excited those in the field of exploration and spurred them on to immediate efforts.

Robert Falcon Scott, a British naval officer and Antarctic explorer, began a dash for the Pole, for he had a hunch that Amundsen was on his way there. The race was on and it was to end in victory and medals for one, in defeat and death for the other.

Captain Scott had a headstart. At the time Amundsen sailed, he was in Australia loading his ship with supplies. When Amundsen realized that Scott was also heading for the South Pole, he cabled him that he had a race on his hands. This civility has frequently been referred to as an act of superb sportsmanship.

The two bases were finally set up—several months later—about four hundred miles from each other. The Amundsen camp was surrounded on all sides by the rearing walls of ice called the Ross Barrier. It was a bleak, sad, drab, windy, and cold spot. Frequently the ship was in danger of being chopped loose from the Barrier, which now and then shattered and broke into gigantic pieces—some of them a mile in length. Sometimes, as well, the Barrier itself went afloat and shifted in the Antarctic Sea.

But Amundsen relied a great deal on his reading. Sir James Ross, after whom the Barrier had been named, noted that several sections could not possibly break loose from the huge Barrier. At the Bay of Whales, an inlet of the Ross Sea, Amundsen moored the *Fram* and boldly made his camp on the Barrier.

Scott, who was one of the world's foremost experts on the Antarctic, established his base aboard his ship and set up a sub-base on a huge floe. The Scott experts were relying on Shetland ponies—those shaggy horses which can withstand cold—to get them to the South Pole. They also had with them several newfangled motorized sledges which could whip along the ice at slow speed. "But they are rugged," Scott told the London press. "Between the Shetlands and the sledges, we will surely make the South Pole in ease and comfort. This is a new age of exploration and a new way of doing it."

Lieutenant Hugh Pennell, who commanded one of the Scott ships, the *Terra Nova*, came to call one day and said that his commander had found dogs to be untrustworthy.

"As you know, sir," the lieutenant said courteously, "our chief is perhaps the greatest expert on Antarctic problems. has found on previous expeditions that dogs are just not to be relied upon at all."

Then he told about the Shetland ponies and the motorized sledges. "We have experimented with them on Scottish moors and we found they were absolutely rugged and unbeatable, sir," the lieutenant said.

Amundsen stroked his beard and nodded. "I disagree. I disagree flatly. I shall be glad to offer half my dogs as a gift to your expedition. Please convey my respects and admiration to your commander and tell him about my offer. I have great confidence in dogs, sir."

The lieutenant thanked Amundsen and said loftily that he was sure Scott would never consider the offer. Hastily he added that Scott would certainly appreciate the warmth of the gesture. "But no, thank you, sir," he said, and sailed away in the *Terra Nova* to chart a coastline.

"Apparently Scott has found much cause for complaint," Amundsen said to one of his dogs while rubbing its ears. "Scott has no faith in you at all. We shall see."

Nor was Amundsen disturbed by the fact that Sir Ernest Henry Shackleton, who was one of the leaders of Scott's expedition, also did not favor the use of Huskies. He had read Sir Ernest's book on his Antarctic explorations and he felt that the great man did not understand dogs or how to use them.

"I don't think they know how to feed you, how to treat you" —here his eyes grew sad—"and how to eat you, if necessary." Then he added, "One thing we know surely. Sir Ernest may be a great explorer, but he doesn't know dogs."

Indeed, it was to be for lack of dogs that Sir Ernest died in 1922 while studying Enderby Land, the vast glacier and land mass fronting on the Indian Ocean in southeastern Antarctica.

Amundsen, however, was "sold" on the Huskies. For one

thing, the dog could eat other dogs, if necessary, while horses depended on cumbersome fodder such as oats, grain, hay, and motorized vehicles needed petroleum—all of which were difficult to transport. He was also sure that the motor sledges and the horses would not be as dexterous as his dogs in scrambling up the sides of icy formations or across narrow icy bridges. The horses and motorized sledges were much heavier and therefore would slip more easily than the dogs, who were reared and trained on ice.

He stroked his beard and wished the Scott expedition well. But he set his dogs to a rigorous course of training, which had been sadly neglected on the long journey from Norway. They were in bad shape, but a good diet of fish, along with exercise and a refresher course in the reins, soon put them in fine fettle. The dogs hardened under Amundsen's kind but firm treatment and soon he had four splendid teams hitched to sleds. He was ready for the dash as soon as the winter had come and gone.

The winter in the Antarctic is far more severe than in the Arctic. As a matter of fact, the Antarctic enjoys the worst weather in the world. But when Amundsen set up his camp at the Bay of Whales he profited once again by the reading he had done. Probably no explorer in history has dissected so minutely what others have written. He made marginal notes in the books he read and then collated the data. When he felt that an explorer-writer was vague about a situation, he noted it. Thus he was able to arrive at solid conclusions which were to stand him in good stead on his historic dash to the Pole.

One conclusion had to do with the site of the base camp. The second justified his reliance on the dogs. The third confirmed his old rule of ample preparation and forethought. All three combined to give him victory.

The *Fram* lacked speed. But she made up for it in ruggedness and power and averaged about one hundred and fifty miles a day. Amundsen selected his site after much thought. They arrived at the Ross Barrier just before the first of the year. It was summertime and sailing was easy. It should be remembered that summer in the Antarctic is winter in the north.

As the *Fram* plowed her way through the Ross Sea, the great ice barrier began to loom in the distance only as a brightening reflection in the sky. The masses of ice ahead of them cast aloft a white sheen that could be seen for miles away. The clouds from afar were whiter and brighter and so was the blue of the sky.

Soon the magnificent wall of ice loomed nearer and the cold grew more intense. The Barrier looked insurmountable as it rose hundreds of feet on all sides, in places rivaling or exceeding the highest skyscrapers in New York City.

Sir James Ross, whose writings Amundsen had carefully studied, noted that one sector of the great Barrier seemed permanent. This was at the Bay of Whales, so named by Shackleton on an earlier expedition. The *Fram* sailed straight into the weird Bay, which was just a deep ring in the vast floating mountain of ice.

When the *Fram* entered, the Bay did not look inviting. The water was somber and choppy; ice floes reared and fell like ships in a heaving sea. However, great iron stakes were driven into the side of the Barrier at its lowest point and a party of crewmen scaled upward to survey the incredible ice plateau. Friendly and unsuspecting seals barked and played in the waters as Amundsen and his small group made their way on skis.

The temperature seemed harmless; the ship below was sheltered; the men were enjoying their first land walk in months, even though they were on skis. Yet Amundsen was uneasy.

He ordered a rope strung from man to man in the party. "It's a new planet," he joked. "Let's stick together."

The alpine file trudged ahead on the barren Barrier looking about them as inquisitely, indeed, as men who reach another planet. They were in a new and different world.

CHAPTER IX

At Longitude Zero

No one can possibly measure the feeling of a man who for the first time stands at the bottom of the earth as it swings in its orbit. Few men have stood there since Roald Amundsen, but those few felt as he did: a sense of awe and exaltation, loneliness and triumph, tiredness and reward. Admiral Richard E. Byrd, who was at the South Pole many years later, felt the same way.

As the earth circled in its orbit, swinging through space, Roald Amundsen lifted his arms and looked up at the stars. Gravity held him to his point at the bottom of the earth's axis. He knew that he was the first man ever to plant his feet there. He wanted to shout; he wanted to kneel and pray. But he forebore for fear of being too dramatic. Always he watched his companions and thought of their reactions, and of the perils that lay ahead of them on their way back to the base camp on the Barrier. He did not want to be ridiculous in their eyes, for they looked to him as their leader.

The dash to the South Pole was undertaken not on the spur of the moment but after months of thought and planning.

Into it went all the years of experience Amundsen had accumulated, plus all the knowledge he had gained from reading about earlier adventures in Antarctica.

When the file of men tied together in alpine fashion started on an exploratory search for a base camp, they hoped to find a site near the edge of the Barrier—one to which supplies could be transferred from the ship without much hardship.

They were lucky. They soon found a little hollow of land on the vast expanse which would shield them against the wind. This spot was selected for the main base and Amundsen plunged a ski stick into the ground to mark it off. They made for the parapet of the Barrier and found to their horror that the ice to which the *Fram* was moored had crumbled. So new stakes were driven in, this time on the plateau of the Barrier. The *Fram* was now held fast and secure to the edge of the ice continent.

Amundsen sat down in the *Fram* and for several days devoted himself to paper work. He had much to do. For one thing, he had to list his forces in terms of men, dogs, food, shelter, and other expendables. No general marshaling his forces has ever done so meticulous a job.

First, he was the nutritionist. He estimated the amount of food required for each man and each dog going to and coming back from the Pole. On this he worked for a full day. He refused to leave to chance the fact that they might kill game en route. Perhaps there would be no game. Perhaps they would lose their weapons. There was no way of telling. So, after calculating to a nicety just what food each man and each dog would need, he worked out a plan for using dog as food. It was not easy.

He was also the navigator, with calculations to make. He

must select the route, and the shorter the better. If he failed to map out the shortest way, a death might occur for which he would be responsible. Into this category came endurance. Which man could travel the longest without cracking?

At this point he became the psychologist. Which men were best fitted, mentally and physically? He set down his observations and his estimates of the men and came to his own conclusions. If he was wrong, someone would suffer; perhaps someone would die.

He then began to consider clothing, weight of the packs, depots . . . needles, bandages, ski sticks, snowshoes, soap, whisky, matches, flags . . . reading material . . . and even an accordion. He smiled as he listed this, but he knew that music was important for the spirit of the men.

Everywhere there lurked danger and death. Precautions must be taken against anything going wrong, for there would be no chance of rescue. The nearest help was a thousand miles distant and there was no way of sending a message to spell out danger.

Actually it was the second time he had worked things out. The first time was back in Norway, after he had decided to go to the South and not the North Pole.

He felt sure that every single expedition to the South Pole had failed because of poor planning. Traveling across ice is an exhausting matter. He who travels lightly, travels best. For this reason Amundsen set down a timetable for the killing of the dogs. It is not a nice story, but it is an understandable one. Either the dogs live while the men die or the dogs die so that the men may live to reach the Pole and return to base. It was as simple as that. Amundsen, the man of the outdoors, loved his dogs. But he loved his men, and his own life, even more. If he was to make the Pole, the dogs would have to be the means—the martyrs to exploration.

He worked silently—mostly on simple arithmetic. He added, divided, and subtracted. So many men, so many dogs, so many depots, so many miles, so much weight, so much food, so much cold, so much clothing. One factor had to balance with the next. When one of his men asked what he was doing, he answered, "I am figuring just what we would need by way of men and power to go to the moon."

The chief reason for the failure of expeditions bent on exploration of dangerous spots was that the entire complex of men and equipment had moved toward the goal. Amundsen planned to use the method which had made possible Peary's discovery of the North Pole. It consisted in establishing a series of bases, of depots which would stretch to the goal, all within marching distance of each other.

"As there are about fifty pounds of edible food in the carcass of an Eskimo dog," he reasoned, "it is quite probable that every dog we take south with us to the Pole will mean fifty pounds less of food to be cached and stored.

"My calculations show the number of dogs I must take on each step to the south, how they must be killed to be used as food for the cache and how they are needed to take the first party back to base.

"The next party must take along a certain number of dogs which can eat the food at the first base, carry the food to the second base, and still supply enough for the men to get back to the main base. Then a third party must take along a certain number of dogs which will be able to live off the first and second base, establish a third base, return to the second and first base and then to the main camp. En route a certain number of dogs must be killed so as to avoid feeding them, avoid taxing them too much, use them for food for the dogs to come and still have enough dog-power left over to take the men back to the main base at the Bay of Whales."

This kind of calculation went on for months. It was cold-blooded, but it was sound. Peary had laid down the rule that the dog must be both the motive power and the food supply. Amundsen was favorably impressed and resolved to follow the idea.

Finally he began to forge his chain of depots. The first party set out with four men and three sleds pulled by batteries of six dogs each. In about five days the team, by reckoning, had made the eightieth meridian of latitude. So clear was the air that on the third day out they could still see the Bay of Whales, although they had averaged about thirty-five or forty miles a day. The visual distance was deceptive and the men felt as though they had covered no ground at all. But the instruments showed that they were approaching the Pole.

The ride back was almost a picnic; for the men allowed the dogs to pull them on the sleds, instead of walking or running alongside. The cache at the first depot had been established. There was enough food in it for the trip to and from the second depot; to and from the third depot, and the fourth depot . . . and for the men who would make the final dash to the Pole and back.

A day after the first team returned, the second team made for the second depot. They ate at the first cache and went on to set up the second depot. On the way back they stopped at the first depot, fared well, and made home base in five days. The following day a third team set out. Each team was led by Amundsen, the iron man who did not rest.

He used his own system of driving the dogs. The Eskimos spread their dogs out fanwise, while the Alaskans used two lead dogs and a double file. Amundsen used his lead dogs, the masters of the pack, on separate traces so that they could nip the flanks of the dogs which refused to work.

He also began to use dried, frozen fish as markers for the routes. Not only did they stand up well in the freezing temperature but they could be used for food going and coming.

When the eighty-first meridian was reached after the third depot had been set up, the temperature according to Amundsen's reading was fifty-two degrees below zero. The time was drawing near for the final spurt to the spot on the bottom of the world.

It was now March in the Antarctic—a month equivalent to October in the North Temperate Zone. There was one major difference, however. While New York or Chicago may feel a fall nip during October, the Antarctic fall, which comes in March, means forty or sixty degrees below zero.

At the fourth depot more than a ton of supplies was laid in the ice and markers were erected. Instruments were tested and a new route was laid out; dogs were killed and rest was taken. On the way back they set frozen fish in the ice, to be used for the next onslaught to the south. Curiously, no animals ate the frozen fish—but, then, there is little game in the Antarctic.

At the next depot—and this one was set up with difficulty and severe hardship—almost a ton of food and supplies was laid in the ice. At the next, a half ton of provisions was laid in. Amundsen was resolved that on the last dash he and his party should not be overloaded with supplies. Overloading was the fatal error, he knew, and at any cost it must be avoided.

April came—and the sun blinked for a moment and vanished as though it were a signal. Then it went away for good. The dark night season fell and remained.

Meanwhile Amundsen had started working on the sleds. He overhauled them so that they were only about a third of their former weight. He used thin, steel runners, a very slender but tough body, and eliminated all the wood he could. The re-design allowed for an additional one hundred pounds in freightage for each sled—a matter that, in terms of food, might make all the difference between death and survival.

Snowshoes and skis were overhauled and repaired. Furs were examined for rips and sewn. Boots and underclothing were gone over, mended, and made watertight. Delicate instruments were checked and rechecked. For, after all, what was the use of trying for the Pole if, when he got there, Amundsen could not be sure he was there?

May, June, July, and August came and went. There was no sun at all—just a dismal night. Once again Amundsen made certain that the depression of the sustained darkness would not lead to dissensions and quarrels. He kept his men busy, stood up to the toughest malcontent, played games with the most somber, took hikes with the most exhausted and lonely, read books to the most jaded, and cooked wonderful meals with the foods in stock and the scanty game and fish he could kill. He never seemed to sleep.

There was much talk in camp about Scott's plans. Were their rivals going to make the dash first? Were they already on their way? Perhaps they had been there and back? Amundsen looked at the sky, at the thermometer, and shook his head. No. It was impossible, he said.

September came and the bubble dropped even lower. It now stood steadily at almost seventy degrees below zero.

Amundsen had met similar cold in the Far North, on the far side of the world; but nothing to equal this, he thought. He wondered whether he was getting old or perhaps losing his resistance. He did not look well, he knew; but he dismissed the thought. He had not looked especially well since that agonizing course through the Northwest Passage.

The cold held. But there was an almost imperceptible change. The sun appeared, glimmered, and vanished. Then it reappeared, only to spark and snuff out again like some guttering candle in a blast of air.

September passed and the cold maintained its grip. But Amundsen was now ready. The sleds were packed; the dogs were in good shape . . . all was at fever pitch. Now and then he made experimental forays for a day or two and returned to camp with a nipped nose or frozen foot. It was good practice, however, and it gave him a chance to work out with the best dogs and the best men—all still experimentally.

October came and the sun glimmered for more than a moment. A fever seized him, a desire to run the race. He became short and somewhat irritable. He stopped eating, and became as gaunt as his Huskies. Some of the men thought he looked like a Husky with his sunken cheeks and bristly beard. At last the day came and he silently went about camp shaking hands. It was October 19, 1911.

They started early in the afternoon. The historic cavalcade of five men, fifty-two dogs, and four sleds mushed out of camp as though they were going on a picnic. Amundsen had a sharp eye out for spirit and supplies. Every bit of equipment had been checked in the morning as to weight and usefulness. He examined the paws of the dogs and their coats. If the fur was good, the health was good. He checked each man's personal equipment. Some of the men thought it was an invasion of their privacy. But he examined each boot, went through each pocket to see that no unnecessary bulk was being taken along. "Preparation, preparation," he muttered apologetically. "That is why I am bothering you."

The dogs strained; the runners broke through the ice; the sleds lurched; the beasts yapped in the crystal air and soon the whole pack was in mournful, operatic cry. The men roared with the release from tension—and off they went. It was perfect, according to plan. "Now we'll see whether the plan is good," Amundsen said to himself. Five lives, including his own, were dependent upon those plans of his that he had charted on paper. Here now was the reality.

The weather held cold and sharp. On the second day two of the dogs were destroyed, thus somewhat spoiling the plan. The pair could not keep up with their mates as they raced along. "Too fat," Amundsen growled. "First mistake."

There were old tracks in the snow. Someone said it must be the Scott party making the dash. Amundsen laughed. "No. Those are yours. You made them six weeks ago when we had a look at the first depot. You turn your skis out like a pigeon. They are your tracks." The men laughed under the dark slate sky. So far, spirits held high.

Soon the clear, frozen terrain changed. The plainlike course was broken with great cracks in the Barrier. They had traversed these while laying out the course for the depots. But now they seemed larger. One of the sleds slipped under a sudden icefall and down it went into a deep abyss. Amundsen seized one of the traces, but two dogs broke free and fell more than thirty feet. However, the trace he held saved the sled. For with presence of mind he wrapped it about a knobby protuberance of ice and threw himself on the ground to hold it fast.

They looked into the crevasse. Sharp, flinty sides of frozen rock made it impossible for anyone to climb down and save the dogs. The sled and the other dogs were practically suspended in mid-air. Amundsen said, "Ice is smooth. If the trace holds, we can pull the whole thing up." The trace did hold, for it was made of the finest Scottish leather.

They heaved at the dead weight, using the thick lump of ice as a kind of pulley. Up and up and up came the sled and up and up came the dogs. Two of the dogs were unconscious, having been caught about their throats in a tangle of the traces. Amundsen looked sadly at them, took out his revolver and shot them dead. He could see they could not recover without nursing care, which would delay the party. And his plan did not brook delay.

One of the men asked jocularly, "Would you shoot one of us if we got hurt and became a burden?"

Amundsen looked at him, his eyes glowing. "Only for disobeying orders or for imperiling the lives of your companions. For these reasons I would shoot any one of you."

"Suppose you got hurt?" the man asked. "And thereby imperiled us?"

"I would command you to shoot me," Amundsen said quietly. "But I hope I would have sense enough to shoot myself so as not to embarrass you."

Amundsen had counted on the two dogs but, like a good general, had made allowances both in men and in dogs for just such a contingency. They pitched camp one night on a smooth, iced-over surface near the first depot. The weather had grown slightly warmer and where they expected thick ice there was just a transparent, thin, coating of it. One of the men actually sank into a crevasse during the night. His cries awakened them and they pulled him out.

The men smiled at the frozen-fish markers and Amundsen said, "They'll be good to eat on the way back. The most intelligent markers I have ever seen. I'm going to apply for a patent on the idea."

The remark was not especially witty, but everyone roared. The excitement of the dash, the eerie sky, the feeling of aloneness, the danger—all combined to make everyone somewhat lightheaded.

One of the men stumbled and almost broke a leg the third day out when his ski tangled with a dog trace. Amundsen, like the general he was, immediately knelt beside the man. "I'll shoot you as I would a dog if you don't get up." He was merely encouraging the man, of course. He would have turned back with the entire party if necessary. After the man had hobbled about a while, the sprain-kinks ironed themselves out and the party was able to proceed. But the one accident might have spelled failure for the whole expedition. It would have meant the end of the adventure had the man broken his leg. They did not have enough supplies to spend another winter waiting for the milder weather. Besides, there was the Scott expedition—which, for all they knew, already had been to the Pole and back.

On the tenth day out, the dogs broke into furious battle. The pack savagely attacked two of the dogs and, despite a heavy laying on of the whip, tore them to shreds. Calmly Amundsen ordered the carcasses packed for dog food. "I counted on this. We have enough dogs to spare," he said. The men looked at him with amazement, but they believed him. They had seen numerous examples of his forethought.

At mealtime they talked incessantly of the Scott party and wondered whether they had been beaten.

"I say no," said Amundsen.

"But look at the equipment, the ships, the supplies, the money," argued one.

"I'm not impressed. They depend on horses in this climate?" he asked scornfully. "On motor sledges? How can they pack all that petrol? Anyhow the motorized sledges are too heavy for the thin ice, when the weather gets better. They'll break through. I predict a calamity."

By the middle of November they came to their fourth depot. The supplies were in good order, and untouched by animals—which, as Amundsen knew from his reading, were almost nonexistent in the Antarctic. Sometimes he jollied the men by telling them that conditions would have been much worse had they gone to find the North Pole. "You're lucky that I took you south for the winter," he said. "This, by contrast to the North, is practically the Riviera."

En route, at each of the depots, the food was carefully parceled out and supervised by Amundsen. "There must be enough left for the trip back. If you eat too much, you'll get fat." The dogs snarled; but he wanted them in lean, gaunt condition, eager and tense, and deliberately he underfed them. "The same holds true of us," he said. "You travel better on a lean belly. It's not true what Napoleon said, that an army marches better on a fat belly."

When the final depot was reached, an incapacity for food overcame him. He felt an inner excitement that dried his mouth. It was the old, familiar feeling he had experienced before in moments of high drama. He lived so fully during these tense days that, as he was accustomed to say in his lectures, it was no wonder he aged rapidly. "I really live fast and the body knows it."

Sometimes, during the final dash, a sadness overcame him. What would he do when he got back? If he made the South Pole, where could he go? "Nothing so tragic as an unemployed explorer," he said ironically. "I will have to go to the moon." But little did he dream what was in store for him later on.

The dash now settled down to a savage pace. They came to a great wash of ice that lifted the frozen Barrier more than three hundred feet into the air. It was difficult and slippery to surmount. But Amundsen, the careful planner, had provided steel pegs which were now driven into the sides, then dogs and sleds and men were hoisted over it. "Preparation, preparation," he muttered. And the men laughed with pleasure and admiration.

There were now eighteen dogs left. All the rest had been destroyed. When he returned to civilization, he was to come in for a great deal of criticism for the calculated slaughter. All kinds of groups devoted to the prevention of cruelty to pets assailed him. They called him a brutal and ruthless man for sacrificing the dogs in order to win the Pole. His answer was the obvious one.

"You slaughter beef cattle for food. We used dogs. That's all." In his opinion the killing of chicken and cattle for human consumption is no less cruel than the killing of dogs. "We killed just as efficiently and with perhaps less pain than is experienced in the stockyards and the barnyards of the world," he said. "We used the swift bullet."

By the end of November they were traversing what is

called the Devil's Glacier. Here the ice was thin and frequently men and dogs and sleds broke through. But Amundsen used mountain-climbing technique. The men were tied
together and rescue was simple. They named this area the
Devil's Ballroom because of the sloughy, slippery path through
which they were practically required to dance their way.

Sometime after the middle of November they had reached
the southernmost point heretofore arrived at by man—the
eighty-eighth parallel. This had been achieved by Shackleton.

According to his reckoning and his estimate of the position
of the Pole, Amundsen was sure they would reach their goal
by December 14. He had pegged his food and endurance estimates to this date.

On the thirteenth he took stock. The men were all in good
health and good spirits. There were fewer dogs than he had
counted on, but these were faring well. The food was in good
supply; the bases behind them were in good order; the weather
was holding and nothing lay ahead of them, as far as the eye
could see, but a smooth, icy tundra with no pitfalls. "It's a
vacation jaunt," he said grimly. The men laughed. They loved
this quiet, shy man who seemed to know just what everyone
needed and when he needed it. He had thought of everything.
There was even a good supply of chocolate and fiery Holland
gin.

December 14 broke and Amundsen felt his heart thump.
He became quite ill when far ahead, on the glassy surface, he
saw mottled snow. "Tracks," he said. "Tracks. It must be the
Scott team." But there were no tracks, just hummocks of snow
blown up by the wind and frozen.

By mid-afternoon Amundsen halted the little group of men
and dogs. The dogs crouched on their hunkers and yapped.

The sky seemed low overhead. Amundsen looked at his watch. "We are two hours late," he said severely. The men laughed nervously and so did he.

He took a shot at the sun with his sextant. "I am more than sure we are at the Pole," he said quietly. The men were over-awed. Amundsen felt tears spring to his eyes, but they were quickly frozen. He could not allow the men to see his emotion.

There were quiet handshakes all around. "Gentlemen," said Amundsen, "we are standing on the bottom of the world. We had planned to stand on top of it, but this is not a bad substitute."

To make sure that he was right, the party circled an area of about ten miles. Then Amundsen halted them, strode to a sled and broke open a package. He unfurled the flag of Norway and planted it solidly in the ice in the name of King Haakon VII. He broke out another package and came up with cigars, which he passed about. The tent was raised and the men sat eating and smoking at the South Pole.

"You must have been pretty sure of the dash to take along cigars," one of the men commented.

"So I was, so I was," Amundsen said smilingly.

"What would you have done with the cigars if we hadn't made it?"

"Smoked 'em," he said laconically.

The next day just to make sure—the men split up in groups and went in several directions with Norwegian flags, which they planted in the ice. "I won't be a minute away from the exact spot," Amundsen said. "This sextant may be excited, too, and not be registering well."

He took frequent shots and, when he felt certain he had

the exact spot, he built a huge pinnacle of snow. On top of this he planted still another Norwegian flag. At the base he left a tent. In the tent were several cigars and a bottle of gin and a note to Scott, who, he thought, might soon be along.

While the men were skirmishing the area picking up small rock souvenirs to take back with them, Roald Amundsen took a deep breath and looked about him with satisfaction. He had done it. He had made the South Pole—the first man to set foot there.

The Scott party reached the tent about a month later, on January 18, 1912. The four men in the party perished on the return journey, and the remains and records of their epic trip were found later.

But Amundsen and his party returned safely after many adventures and moments of danger. He wept unashamedly, later on, when news of Scott's death reached him. "Perhaps he was dispirited on his way back knowing that I had been there first. Perhaps that is what caused his death. I will never know, of course," he wrote in a letter. "But I feel badly for this great man."

CHAPTER X

The Ginx of the Maud

Ninety-nine savage days passed and almost two thousand miles of perilous territory were traversed before Amundsen and his party returned safely to the *Fram*.

On the way back, several of the dogs on which they had counted were killed in sudden, snarling brawls. The Huskies were beginning to crack under the long trek and almost hourly slashed at one another or banded up and fell on a lone victim and cut him to ribbons. Some of the dogs even deserted and made their way north, where the explorers later found evidence that they had broken into the food caches at the depots.

One sled was lost when it fell into a crevasse, while another, just as on the way down to the Pole, was barely saved from a sudden opening in the great ice plain. The dogs dragged it along on a broken runner.

"Happy New Year!" Amundsen shouted to the men as they were recrossing Devil's Glacier. It was New Year's Day. While the rest of the world was celebrating the holiday by their own firesides, the doughty group brought in the New Year by munching on pemmican and washing it down with fiery gin.

Dawn was breaking on January 25 when, with only eleven dogs in the traces, the victorious party arrived at the Bay of Whales. The base was deserted and Amundsen was furious to see that the *Fram* was nowhere in sight. He had left orders for it to stay out the period in Buenos Aires, where it was to take on provisions. He had missed his return date by only twelve hours, so detailed had been his planning and preparation.

However, the men made themselves comfortable in the hut on the Barrier and found it reasonably well supplied with coffee, biscuits, and tinned foods. They sat down to wait out the return of the *Fram*. But they didn't have long to wait, for on the following day they saw a sail on the horizon. The *Fram* had been delayed by a gale.

Amundsen was now eager to tell the world of the successful dash. All remaining stores were packed aboard and the *Fram* beat her way north to civilization. The crew of the *Fram* had no word of the Scott Expedition, but they did bring a letter from the Australian Antarctic Expedition that said it would be glad to purchase any dogs or supplies Amundsen would like to sell. He felt particularly happy about his few remaining dogs, for he had been in a quandary as to what to do with them. Their natural habitat was the frozen world and he was glad that they would have work to do for another assault on the Antarctic.

At Hobart, Tasmania, which lies southwest of Australia, Amundsen went ashore, followed by a curious group of natives. The bearded, craggy-faced stranger sought out a local official, asked to be allowed to send a telegraph message to Norway, and said he had discovered the South Pole. The official was polite but disbelieving. "The Scott Expedition, our own British explorer, must have done so," he declared. "We have not heard from him as yet, but we are sure he got there before you did."

Amundsen snorted but filed his story. In a few hours, messages of congratulations came pouring in from Continental Europe and America. However, the Royal Society of England said sharply and tersely, "We will wait to hear from Scott. His expedition was well equipped, while this adventurer who was supposed to have gone to the North Pole and claims to have wound up at the South Pole could not possibly have done it."

Almost nine months later—no word had been heard from the Scott party—a rescue expedition found Scott's own diary in which he had written: "The worst has happened, or nearly the worst. I am disappointed for my loyal companions, but I give Amundsen all credit and homage. He arrived before we did and left us a message."

Then he added: "It is an awful place and terrible enough for us to have labored to it without the reward of being the first." Scott's end must have been frightful for, according to his diary, he was the last member to be left alive. All about him were his dead companions and dead ponies. They had starved to death.

During the next few years Amundsen was awarded magnificent honors by several governments and many scientific organizations. The great National Geographic Society of the United States bestowed a gold medal upon him, while universities vied with one another in awarding him degrees. Several societies and foundations granted him cash prizes.

Rarely did he dine alone. Life became crowded with banquets and receptions. His knowledge of languages was slight;

but because he had read, with the aid of dictionaries, so many accounts of explorations written in other tongues, it was soon fairly easy for him to give presentable addresses. He was now considered second only to Peary among the world's foremost living explorers.

Often, when the weather outside his lavish hotel suite was frosty, he smiled a small-boy smile and bared his chest to the wind in remembrance of his self-training period when he was a foolish, romantic boy.

Several British textbook firms were so sure that Scott had discovered the South Pole that they had rushed into print with articles on their national hero. Many years were to pass before this error was expunged, for a large number of the books had been sold to schools. Now and then Amundsen met Britons who looked at him doubtfully. They had read the erroneous stories about Scott but had not heard of his failure and death. But, of course, Amundsen is today the acknowledged discoverer of the South Pole.

His lecture tours throughout Europe and the United States brought him a great deal of money. He did not especially enjoy making speeches unless he was addressing learned men who understood polar conditions. However, it was the fashionable groups, and not the scientific ones, that paid high admission fees to hear him speak. Sometimes he became impatient and blunt when people asked him questions after a lecture.

For example, one well-meaning lady inquired, "What would you have done if you and your dogs were starving?"

"Madame," he said grandly, "I would have eaten my dogs unless they got at me first."

This sort of response, which he meant honestly, was not well received in many quarters, but he did not care. He was telling the truth about the rigors of polar exploration and he did not intend to mince words. Mostly, though, the listeners loved the rugged man with the lined face who talked haltingly about the bottom and the top of the world. He spoke with a love and a passion that somehow caught them up in the wonderful adventure of seeking out the unknown, and they went home feeling that they had participated in the romance of the barking dogs, the rigorous frost, the perils, and the taste of pemmican—all of which he had managed to impart. "We'll tell our grandchildren about this," many said to him, "for we shook the hand of the man who discovered the South Pole."

Other men would have been content, after receiving the plaudits of the world, to stay home and write books or lecture. He could have enjoyed a lifelong income as an instructor at any of the great universities. Or he might have retired on the tens of thousands of dollars he had earned from his lecturing. But he looked upon money and fame as just another springboard to the polar seas. He sat down and began to plan another expedition.

It was now 1914. The *Fram* was in Norway being fitted out for his drifting excursion to the North Pole. He kept pouring out money to the shipbuilders and provisioners. He gazed into the air and from it he obtained still another idea. He would explore by air. So he purchased an old Farman biplane and planned to leave room for it on the *Fram's* deck. He began to read books on air piloting and air navigation.

He dreamed of taking the *Fram* up north and allowing her to drift while he made side excursions in the biplane to survey the icy masses and waters about the North Pole. He inquired about ski-runners for take-offs and landings. He also drew his own designs for heating the interior of the cabin.

The plane itself was a crude affair—struts, a small, coughing motor, and flimsy wings. He wondered whether it could stand up against the great, sweeping Northern gales which smashed at anything in their path. He smiled grimly and thought he would take a chance. He began to take flying instructions at a small airport near Oslo. He was now forty-two years old; he had made his mark in history, but he was still learning and dreaming.

Because of his fame, many rich men were glad to supply him with funds for his next expedition in the hope that a newly discovered bay, sea, island, peninsula, or cape might be named after them. Amundsen was not averse to the idea but accepted their money without committing himself.

He now had his ship, his plane, and the funds he needed. But history was moiling up and in Europe the first of the great world wars was in the making. Across the Continent marched the forces of the German Kaiser and the world was horror-stricken. For many years, statesmen, historians, editorial writers had been saying that war would never again break out. Except for a nasty flurry in the Balkans and a colonial war in South Africa, men the world over were sure that civilization had reached the point where nations would no longer resort to war.

World War I broke with all its fury and millions of men, practically all of them on foot, fought one another on two great European fronts. Famine and devastation were horrible, and perhaps more widespread than at any other time in the long centuries of strife. For the first time, civilians became victims of battle. Although Norway remained neutral, Amundsen decided to wait out the fury before going off on another trip.

He went into the shipbuilding business with the idea of earning money with which to finance his future explorations. Norway, a peaceful nation, was now building ships for the West to replace the bottoms which were being sunk by German submarines. At first Amundsen was of two minds about the colossal struggle. He favored neither side but blamed both. He felt sure that peace could have been made before the first cannon was fired and the first soldier killed.

Too, he saw no terror in the German U-boat warfare. He thought it made little difference whether a ship was sunk by a shell fired from another ship, a bomb dropped from a plane, or a volley fired from coastal batteries. But when the Germans, after sinking a ship, surfaced in their U-boats and machine-gunned human beings floating helplessly in lifeboats, he became furious. He knew what it meant to flounder at the mercy of the sea without the additional horror of being shot at.

He threw his sympathies in with the Allies and, in an action which forever endeared him to the West, he phoned the German Embassy in Oslo asking for an appointment.

He came in bearing a heavy briefcase. "I come to tell you that I am returning all the honors your barbaric nation has bestowed upon me," he told the astounded Ambassador. Then he dumped on the desk all the gold medals, diplomas, scrolls, and testimonials which he had received from numerous German universities and scientific societies. "Inform these groups that, if they are supporting this vicious form of warfare, I relinquish any honors they have given me. They are not worthy of presenting me with honors.

Amundsen's gesture brought him an invitation from the United States Government to visit the Western Front as an observer, an honor accorded to very few foreigners.

By this time—it was 1917—he had earned from his ship-building enterprise almost a quarter of a million dollars. Only for a fleeting moment did he think of retiring. A mere glance at his fur hood, his skis, his Eskimo souvenirs, his caribou boots, and at the snow flaking his window, and he changed his mind. For a while he had thought of devoting the rest of his like to making scientific experiments with tides or weather or to studying the effects of the Magnetic Pole on seamanship and navigation. But after looking at his beloved furs he smiled ruefully and knew he was a lost man. He knew his place was on the ice fields.

"I must have ice in my veins," he told his relatives and his housekeeper. His brothers were furious with him. "We can all do well. Why sell out your business?" they demanded.

But he would have none of business. "I can't sit at a desk for the rest of my life. I am bored with it. I can't have lunch with businessmen and talk contracts. I want to do what I have to do. And I have enough money to do it with. I am the happiest man in the world, for I have done what I always hoped to do and I'll continue to do what makes me happiest."

His housekeeper, a woman of practical and romantic turn, tried to get him interested in marriage. "You want sons and daughters. You are rich and famous. Just look at what you can do for them and for a good woman. You will be happy."

For a while he was interested in a beautiful young widow. He took her to restaurants, bought her gifts, and even proposed to her. She was very much in love with him, and he with her. But it did not work out. Often, when she wanted him to have lunch with her family, he preferred to show her his *Maud,* a new ship being built for him at the famous Christian Jensen shipyard. He paid more attention to the *Maud* than to her. "Look at the fine wood; the unusual design; the way she responds, even in dry dock, to the tiller," he said.

But the beautiful woman would have none of it. "You're an iceman," she said, and immediately married another man.

Amundsen sat at the window and looked out at the ice and snow and agreed that he was a man accursed. "I'll go back to the ice," he told himself. "I can't live in a home and be a domesticated animal." And so it was to be for the rest of his life.

He was never to know the companionship of a woman or the joy of children, the warmth of his own fireplace or the pleasures of normal living. He knew only, until his end, the lure of the Far North and the Far South, the sharp bite of the wind, the treachery of the ice, or the heave of a vessel beneath his feet. He stormed into the face of danger when he could have relaxed with the surety that he had already made his mark.

During the war, while turning out ships for money, he was using his profits to build a vessel for himself. The *Maud,* as he christened her, took a year to fashion. Her lines were so unusual that seafaring men came from many ports just to look at the strange shape of the vessel.

"She was not planned for a pleasure yacht," he said, grinning. "I laid her out with a definite purpose in mind."

The entire hull was rounded so that she would not be snagged in shallows or be gripped by ice. Her curved sides resembled archways, which are intended to support heavy structures. These contours would withstand the formidable pressure of ice packs that closed in and squeezed like giant nutcrackers. Amundsen got the idea for the rounded surfaces from the ancient Greek and Roman architects who by use of the curve were able to put up huge temples without fear that they would fall down. On June 4, 1917, she went down the ways in Oslo. Queen Maud of Norway, after whom she was named, attended the launching ceremony.

Amundsen had spent a fortune constructing and outfitting his ship. She was one hundred and twenty feet long with a beam of forty feet. Her timbers were imported from Holland, her spars from Portugal, and her rigging from England. Tins of food and sides of bacon, in ton quantities, were especially ordered from the United States. He purchased nothing but the finest clothing for his crew; much of it was tailored in Norway from his own designs.

The *Maud* slipped out of Tromsö, in the northern part of Norway, and soon entered the Barents Sea. It was July 15, 1918. He was glad to get away from what he called a "savage world at war" and into a "kinder one where men only faced the natural and kinder elements."

The crew was nervous about the submarines, which at that time did not discriminate between belligerents and neutrals. So anxious were the Germans to keep supplies out of enemy countries that they torpedoed a ship on sight without caring what flag it flew. Chances are that the Germans would not have minded sinking the *Maud*, for Amundsen had personally affronted Kaiser Wilhelm by returning a decoration the monarch had pinned on him at a ceremony in Berlin. As a matter of fact, Norwegian officials had warned him that it would be wise to get a guarantee of safe passage from the Imperial German Government before trying to sail the Arctic. But he refused. "Mine is a vessel devoted to peaceful and scientific pursuits. Any nation that orders its submarines to attack it is a barbarous nation."

A few days out, in the White Sea, he was astounded when all hands appeared on deck wearing life belts and carrying their possessions. They had been called for sail duty and thought an alarm had been sounded. He lectured the men severely. "We are at war with no one but storms and the ice. Meantime we have a storm on our hands. Let's fight it."

The *Maud* beat her way easterly through the well-charted Northeast Passage across the top of the world. Though the Passage was frozen in for a good part of the year, it had been used for centuries as a regular shipping route between northern Russia and the Scandinavian countries. He had never been through it and, adventurer that he was, he decided to try it. Naturally he had read up on the Passage and studied hundreds of charts before setting sail. He was sure that this route to the Arctic was not only shorter but also safer from the threat of submarines than the North Atlantic would be.

But there seemed to be a curse on the *Maud*. One incident after another occurred to make Amundsen wonder whether, in spite of his seasonal background, he was losing his control. Here he had a new ship, a competent crew, plenty of supplies, yet mishap after mishap occurred. Though he loved all ships and especially the *Maud*, for she was his very own, he began to distrust her soon after they had put to sea.

Skirting the Arctic Ocean, they passed through the Kara Sea above the Yamal Peninsula, where they encountered several fierce storms. At Dickson Island they took on fresh water and gasoline and by early September they were passing above Cape Chelyuskin, the northernmost promontory of the great Asiatic mainland.

The ice thickened and crept closer. The channels became narrower and the cold grew ever fiercer. They sought shelter on the southerly side of two tiny islands but found it difficult beating up to the lee because of the fierce winds and the encroaching ice. However, they managed to moor just a few hundred yards from the beach and here they were to stay for almost a year.

As usual the first preparations were made for the observatory instruments and the dogs. At last the crew could think of themselves—and then Amundsen had the first of his series of accidents.

It happened on the runway leading up to the *Maud*.

Out of tons of snow shoveled by hand they had built a kind of icy gangplank running to the shore, and along either side they had constructed a railing by standing skis in a row and joining them with a rope knotted about the top of each. One day the explorer was going down the icy gangplank when one of the dogs bounded up, ran between his legs, and tripped him. He fell heavily and broke a shoulder bone.

The bone healed slowly in the freezing weather. Moreover, it had been improperly set and he was in constant, excruciating pain—the worst he had ever experienced. An X-ray some years later showed a very wide fracture that had knitted poorly. But he was not yet done with the bad shoulder.

A month later, at early dawn, he stepped off the ship and went down the gangplank to visit one of the observation huts where the instruments were at work. He heard a heavy panting in the white stillness on shore. Then with a frightened yapping, one of the dogs ran like a startled hare up the runway, turned, and snarled defiance into the gloom.

And out of the murky shadows came a huge white bear

on all fours, furious and grunting. That was the panting he had heard. Alongside her trotted a whimpering cub which apparently had been teased by the Husky.

The bear looked at Amundsen and Amundsen looked at the bear. Even if he had been armed, he wouldn't have tried a shot at such close quarters. A wounded bear can be a raging tornado. And she was raging enough as it was.

She came closer, snuffling and grunting and waving her great paws. She was perhaps eight or nine feet tall. The cub echoed her threats.

Casually Amundsen started for the gangplank and the ship —"as though I wanted to get a cup of coffee," he said later in telling of the adventure. But the bear didn't like his nonchalance and advanced on him. He walked faster and she shambled along after him. He began to run, made the gangplank; but she was right behind him, hot breath, great paws, and all.

Suddenly she swung with the paw and struck his bandaged shoulder. He fell heavily. The pain seared like a red-hot poker. The bear began to maul him but, luckily, was distracted by other game.

The Husky, seeing the bear hesitate, dashed down the gangplank and made for the cub. The bear snarled and turned away from Amundsen, who lay prone on his back shouting, and shambled rapidly after the Husky, which made off across the white wastes.

The shouting and snuffling and yapping had meantime attracted help. But Amundsen was in bad shape and stayed in his bunk for two weeks. He considered himself lucky to be alive. The Husky was so badly frightened that it didn't return until the next day.

No sooner was he up and around and ready to take charge again than he tripped and fell down a small companionway. Again the fractured shoulder was wrenched and he suffered severe contusions. This time he was incapacitated for three more weeks.

Frequently he laughed as he thought of the stories he was going to tell during his lecture tours—"if I ever get back alive," he said. "I've had more accidents and more trouble on the *Maud* than during all my years of exploration."

But his adventures on the ill-fated *Maud* were far from over. He was set to drift to the Pole, if possible, and this adventure was to be one of the most colorful episodes of his colorful life.

CHAPTER XI

The Frozen Fist

It was months before Amundsen could lift his right arm again, hold a pen, lace his boots, or wash himself. Defying the pain, he deliberately put himself through daily exercises. His shoulder improved, but it was never really good again. Then he had another accident and this affected his heart for the rest of his life.

After taking readings in one of the little observation huts which was tightly sealed to keep out light, he turned off the instrument but forgot to open one of the push-windows and light the vapor lamp. Soon he became sleepy and he was almost asphyxiated by the kerosene fumes. Just in time, he realized something was happening to him and broke out of the door in a mad scramble for air. The following week, when he felt well enough to climb a hummock of ice he discovered that his heart was pumping at an unusually rapid rate and that he was short of breath. The close call with death had left him with heart trouble.

The jinx on the *Maud* held. Spring came and went, but the thaw and breakup failed to materialize. The ship was still held in the grip of winter and the ice refused to crumble and crack. But less than half a mile away they could see open, blue sea.

With a pang Amundsen recalled Dr. Cook and his brilliant, if cumbersome, method of cracking the ice ahead of them when, years ago in the Antarctic, they were held fastbound in the *Belgica*. The poor man, Amundsen thought to himself. His old friend and mentor was now held in disrepute the world over because scientific societies had declared him a charlatan and a fraud for claiming that he had reached the North Pole.

Years later when he passed through Kansas on a lecture tour Amundsen stopped off to see Cook at the Fort Leavenworth penitentiary, where the noted explorer was serving a sentence for land swindles. The once-energetic doctor was now a pale and haunted ghost and wept with gratitude when he saw his former shipmate. "They are liars; they are jealous. I did make the Pole. Believe me, Roald," he cried. Amundsen, disregarding the outburst, hastened to comfort the broken, ruined man. And he left a sum of money with the prison authorities for extra food and tobacco for his old friend.

Such an act of kindness, such devotion to an old friend is a rare thing among public figures, who must guard their reputations and seldom have anything to do with former friends who have fallen. But Roald Amundsen had an almost pathological sympathy for those in distress, no matter how much he did or did not like them. This feeling, later on, was to lead to his loss and death.

Here, off northern Siberia, there was but one thing to do—and that was to utilize Dr. Cook's old method of breaking a way through the ice.

The whole crew turned out to drill and chop and gash holes into the ice at various intervals until the open water was reached. This time, remembering what had happened on the *Belgica* when the ice closed over the channels, Amundsen had great wads of cloth placed in the openings. These wads were easily tugged out when they were no longer needed.

The work went on for weeks. Then, when the chopping was completed, great charges of dynamite were placed in each hole and hooked up with a large battery and with wires that led to the ship. Amundsen pushed down the plunger . . . there was a thundering explosion which echoed and re-echoed across the barrier, and ice and water spumed high in the air. The Huskies barked and screamed and fled at the din.

When everything settled down, they saw that the ice was still holding fast. But Amundsen was not disheartened, for his charts told him that high tide was usual in the area on September 12. He felt sure that the uprushing waters would swell the cracks made by the dynamite and force open the ice. He relates that the night of watching was the most beautiful of his life.

There suddenly appeared in the sky the aurora borealis—the magnificent, luminous display of lights that stream down fanwise from the north and light up the world about them in shades that, as he put it, "break the heart." The crew stood on the deck transfixed and humbled, silent and awe-stricken as the lights played across the sky and were reflected in the waters and the ice-locked land.

In the distance, under the colorful blaze, polar bears and their cubs gamboled on the ice as though they were bathing in the bright reflection. Soon, as though in symphony with the lights, there came a grumbling, crashing, and heaving and the ice parted. "Like the Red Sea when Moses parted the waters at the direction of God," Amundsen said. And the swell of the tide did loosen the ice, and the ship, sails furled, made its way through.

Some days previously two men had started back home. One of them complained about severe headaches and the other, who was homesick, decided to accompany him. Amundsen gave them ample clothing and provisions and they set off on the ice to Dickson Island, about five hundred miles away. They never made it. Sometime later one body was found, but the other never was. Whether they had separated after losing their food in a crevasse, or whether one had taken ill and died and the other wandered off alone, will never be known. But tragedies such as these are not rare in the lonely and savage wastes of the world.

The *Maud's* freedom was of short duration. Eleven days later, beyond Cape Shelasky, the ice again closed in rapidly and they were jammed in it off Aijou Island for still another year's stay. The ice pack refused to crack and there was nothing to do but wait out the will of the Arctic.

While idling in the ice, Amundsen dreamed of a ship that could crunch the great blocks ahead. Often he sketched what such a ship would look like and many of his designs have been utilized by ship architects of the United States, Norway, and Soviet Russia. But his goal was still far away and he was almost beside himself with impatience. Two years and little to show for them except scientific observations of the Magnetic Pole, which he was still trying to fix; notes about the habits of polar bears; general memorandums on drift, current, and ice. The endless night came in and the sun was a thing remembered.

The *Maud* was jinxed—of that he was sure, after the second long night had passed and they reached Nome, Alaska. They had made a small circle across the forehead of the world and had got no place at all. There were a few compensations. One of the crew members, Dr. Peter Sverdrup, went on a side expedition with Siberian aborigines, the Tsjuktsji Eskimos, and traveled with them across the ice to their main base, where he stayed with them for six months before returning to the *Maud*. He brought back wonderful notes about their social customs which were later embodied in an important book.

A second good result was that Amundsen had his shoulder looked at by a competent doctor—something he could not have done had they made the Arctic Ocean and plunged ahead to the North. The doctor said that the shoulder needed resetting and that Amundsen required at least two or three months in the hospital. He would not hear of it, especially after four crew members decided they had had enough of the ice and asked to be paid off at Nome. They wanted to work their way down the coast and get back to Europe. He did not blame them, he said.

The *Maud* left Nome and rounded Cape Dog's Head, as it is called. Here they broke a propeller and were forced to winter again in a bleak spot. It was now the third year of failure. But at no point, although he felt frustrated, did Amundsen speak of giving up his future on ice. Dozens of other men similarly confronted with an abortive voyage, when everything had promised so well, would have thrown in the sponge and called it a day and rested on their laurels. Instead, Amundsen looked about the dismal landscape and found something of interest.

He practically took up living with the Tsjuktsji so that he could the better study their social customs and religious beliefs; their simple, primitive laws; their folk chants, fears, and so on. So attached did the tribe become to him that, when it was time to sail south again, he took five natives along with him to Seattle, where he planned to have the *Maud* inspected and overhauled after her three years in the giant icebox.

He was not surprised that the five, who made very good sailors and caught on quickly to lucid instruction, wrinkled their noses at civilization. They thought Western man was crazy to live in such close and filthy quarters. They shook their heads incredulously at the crowded streets, the bustle, the breakneck automobiles, and the poor manners of people who hurried by without greeting one another. Amundsen laughed and said that they probably learned more about the white man during their few days in Seattle than he had learned about the Tsjuktsji after a year with them.

He paid them off and arranged for their return passage north, where they could make their way overland back to their tribe and their own "better" civilization. However, he took two Eskimo children—both girls—to Norway for their education and promised their parents he would see that they returned safe and well. He had formed a close attachment to the sailing youngsters and he was anxious, moreover, to study the effect of modern schooling on the primitive mind.

He saw the girls safely registered in school, then went about trying to raise money with which to purchase a plane to use in connection with his scheme to drift the *Maud* across the Arctic Sea. His vast fortune, which he had earned so rapidly building ships, had vanished on the construction of the *Maud* and her futile voyage.

He had not been in Norway an hour when he learned, to his astonishment, that during his absence his government had voted him a sum of five hundred thousand kroner with which to "advance man's geographical and scientific knowledge of the polar regions." This spontaneous act of the Norwegian Parliament, passed without his knowledge or request, touched him deeply and made him realize the warm feeling his fellow countrymen had for him.

But he was always to be dogged by insufficient funds. Unfortunately, in the financial convolutions that followed the war, the krone had dropped to half its former value, and the appropriated sum was now worth only about seventy-five thousand dollars.

But it would suffice for his purposes. He had his eye on a Junker plane which, according to reports, could stay aloft for a full day or longer. He was resolved to use such a plane to study Arctic weather. It was well known that the world's weather was "made" in the polar areas. So in the interest of better forecasting and for the purpose of studying the influence of weather on shifting seasons, which meant so much to agriculture and the world's food supply, he planned a series of fast dashes by air. The principle was the same as Nansen's formula of fast dashes by dog sled. Amundsen was now to pioneer polar exploration and scientific study by air, after traversing the region for so long on foot.

He purchased a Junker in New York and made arrangements to have it sent to Seattle. Meantime he met a Mr. C. M. Keys who headed the Curtiss Aviation Company of Long Island. Keys became very enthusiastic about the explorer and generously presented him with a light Oriole made by Curtiss for reconnaisance flights in the Arctic. This, too, was sent on short hops to Seattle to join the *Maud*.

While in New York, Amundsen grimly went to see a heart specialist who confirmed what a great London doctor had told him a few weeks earlier. His heart was bad, the specialist declared. "No more explorations for you," he said, echoing his British colleague. "You must get into an armchair and take it easy." Amundsen was fifty years old and the prospect of rocking in a chair, as he put it, horrified him. He paid no attention to the physicians and blithely went on his way. If he was to die, he wanted to die happily and not sit it out.

The *Maud* took on provisions for seven years. This was his answer to the doctors. He had the planes transferred by schooner and just a few months later, on foot, he made a dash of five hundred miles through the snow with a mail carrier at the rate of about fifty miles a day. During the next six days he plowed through more than three hundred miles of snow. This, as well, was his answer to the doctors. He never felt better, though his heart palpitated. "However, I don't palpitate, which is the important thing," said the weather-beaten man.

While in Norway he had fired Lieutenant Jan Omdal of the Royal Norwegian Air Force with enthusiasm for polar flying and exploration. The stocky young lieutenant came along with him and helped set up the Junker for its rugged flying future. Skis supplanted the wheels and, a few days after he returned from a trek inspecting the ice to the west and north, Amundsen took the Junker up for a trial spin.

It flew beautifully enough, but landing the heavy plane on steel runners was another matter. As it came in, a runner was badly twisted. Another was put on and this time the sheer weight of the craft smashed both runners. Omdal suggested pontoons. "We can always land on water," he said.

"Sometimes there is no water for many, many miles," Amundsen said. "However, let's try pontoons." These were put on and the Junker came skimming in like a bird, hit the water—and the impact sent both pontoons flying off. The Junker was impracticable, for it was much too heavy.

Amundsen now thought of a Dornier, the graceful plane especially made for taking off and landing on water. The Dornier company was very anxious to sell him one of their flying boats at a reduced price in return for the publicity they would get. Meantime the Junker firm offered to give him a brand-new Junker free, for the same reason. But Amundsen was doubtful now that a heavy plane could be trusted to do the job.

Because of lack of money, he entrusted his purchasing affairs to a fellow countryman who lived in Seattle and was supposed to be a good businessman. This man bought not one but three Dorniers on credit. He also went about selling a scheme of flying postcards over the Pole and canceling them en route, with the new Amundsen Expedition acting as post-masters.

When Amundsen came to Seattle to inspect the Dornier and found three flying boats with heavy bills attached, he was furious. Moreover, he soon learned of the undignified and foolish schemes of his business agent, whom he summarily fired. But he was now heavily in debt, for the Dorniers had come to more than one hundred and twenty thousand dollars. In addition, his agent had made other purchases—many thousands of dollars worth—in the name of the famous Amundsen.

The jinx on the *Maud*, his beautiful and specially built ship, still held. Amundsen called this entire period of his life "the frozen fist." He said, "First I was held on the ice by the freeze and then I was held by my creditors."

When Amundsen could not meet his debts, the old story of how he had sailed away on the *Gjoa,* leaving his creditors standing on the dock, was revived. A few years back, when the world hailed him for negotiating the Northwest Passage and for discovering the South Pole, this story had been written up in the newspapers with affection. Everyone had laughed at his temerity and youthful impudence. Genially this incident was overlooked and put down to intrepid spirit.

But now that he had been stuck in the ice for three years and had accomplished nothing spectacular since then—and, moreover, had run up debts—the world turned against him. He was assailed on all sides and he became a bitter man. Even some of the Norwegian newspapers attacked him for "biting off more than he could chew." The press advised him to clear his debts and settle down. "There are no more worlds to conquer," it said.

He returned to Norway in an attempt to seek help from former well-wishers and friends who had banqueted him and cheered him. But he was yesterday's hero, a forgotten man. There were new heroes today. Besides, he was poor and heavily in debt. King Haakon VII was still his friend but could not help him. "Go back to America," the King said. "There's a great deal of money there and you can earn it on a lecture tour."

But meantime his creditors were at him like wolves. Even one of his brothers—and this was the bitterest blow—brought suit against him. His brother Leon, who had been managing his personal affairs for him, now said that Roald was in debt to him personally for twenty-five thousand dollars. The explorer who had never been beaten by the most howling gales now succumbed to the financial storm. He went into bankruptcy, his home near Oslo was seized, and he was without means of livelihood.

With the help of the few friends he had left, the somber man returned to the United States to go on a lecture tour. But here, as well, he was yesterday's hero. Audiences did not cram the lecture halls to hear him speak about experiences which had been told before. He felt the ignominy of even having to appear on platforms to earn money for further services to men and the world they inhabit.

He went from coast to coast, but no one was able to drum up any enthusiasm for him or for what he had to say. There were times when he thought wildly of going to the frozen North and living with the Eskimos. It seemed a sad thing to him that he was compelled to stand on a platform like a "mountebank" and perform for the perfumed ladies and their stay-at-home husbands. His contempt knew no bounds. He felt sick to think that men like himself—men, who had been given the accolades of the world's great universities and societies, cities and governments; who had been treated with parade and pomp, banquets and flattery—should now be reduced to poverty and disgrace.

It was during this period that he visited the dishonored Dr. Cook in prison and left for him some of his meager store of funds.

He returned to New York and waited in his hotel room for the ship that was to take him back to Norway. No one phoned him. The newspapers shunned him, whereas formerly the reporters had thronged to interview him. He trudged the winter streets, looked at the sky, and again wished he were back in the North with people who knew nothing of money. He thought idly of going back into business and recouping his losses, but he shuddered at the thought. He knew he would rather die of starvation than sit at a desk and haggle over money.

He sat in his room defeated and broken. "Ah," he said, "maybe I'm getting old. Maybe I've done my job and the world is wise for by-passing me."

The phone rang. Must be a New York creditor I don't know about, he thought, hesitating. Again the phone rang. He picked it up. "Hello," he said.

"Hello," the voice replied. "I'm Lincoln Ellsworth."

CHAPTER XII

Aloft and Down in the White Waste

When the tall, thin, smiling man with the good face and classic features strode into Amundsen's room, his hand outstretched, his manner deferential and eager, a whole new phase of the explorer's life was ushered in. It seemed as though he was starting anew. After thirty years of triumph on foot he was to realize his dream of polar charting by air.

"I am honored to meet you, sir," said Ellsworth.

"Thank you," said Amundsen.

Ellsworth was a man with a large, private income. He came from a family that had made a huge fortune from land and machinery. He had been touched by the magic of the North on several trips to Alaska, and he had made a voyage to the South Pacific. He had read about Amundsen's difficulties and was hopeful, he said, that he could help. "I am diffident about approaching you."

It was like a miraculous visitation. He had been sitting in despair and here, like a bolt from the blue, was the answer to his problem.

"I should like to supply some money for another expedition," said Ellsworth. "May we discuss it?"

"Discuss it, my boy. You're the answer to my problems," said Amundsen. "I will be frank with you. I'm at my wit's end. You sit right down here and make yourself comfortable."

Soon the two were in animated conversation. Fascinatingly enough, Ellsworth's idea of an expedition was the very thing Amundsen had been planning for years—a flight across the Arctic Ocean. They agreed to share the command and whatever glory there would be. Amundsen was to supply the experience, which Ellsworth said he badly needed. "I would hate to be set down in the middle of nowhere without a seasoned leader such as you," he said. And Amundsen needed the money. "I could not be set down in the middle of nowhere without your funds," said the explorer jocularly.

They talked far into the night, shook hands, and arranged to meet the following day for lunch.

When Amundsen awakened early in the morning after only two hours of sleep, he shook his head in wonderment. "Was I dreaming?" he asked. He was not dreaming, but because he was practical he made a few telephone calls to check on the visitor's claims. They needed very little confirmation. The man was rich, adventurous, and of good character. Only eight years younger than Amundsen, he presented a far more youthful appearance simply because he had led a more sheltered life, though he had hunted wild game in Africa, Asia, and South America. "He's a good fellow and a good sportsman," a newspaperman told Amundsen.

And he was. During the next few short years the pair never had a falling-out about anything. Ellsworth deferred to

Amundsen and always insisted that the explorer get "top billing" in any publicity or honors that came their way.

The new partner agreed to provide some eighty-five thousand dollars in cash. This was to go for the purchase of two Dornier-Wal seaplanes, the very same type that Amundsen's ruinous agent had purchased for him on credit.

Amundsen sought out two excellent pilots, First Lieutenants Hjalmer Riiser-Larsen and Leif Dietrichsen of the Royal Norwegian Navy. The four met at Spitsbergen, a huge Norwegian island at the rim of the Arctic Ocean, in May of 1925. The two Dorniers were throbbing just outside the door of the hut in which they were talking. But the N-24 and N-25, as the two planes were designated, were not the main topic of conversation.

Riiser-Larsen dropped a bombshell at the meeting by announcing casually that an airship called the N-1 could be purchased for a song from the Italian Government. The man to contact, he said, was Colonel Umberto Nobile. In the meantime he suggested: "How about making a plane flight just as a reconnoitering expedition to see what it's like from upstairs?"

Amundsen's eyes lit up. "We can soon find out whether an airship can stand up under the buffeting," he said.

Ellsworth smacked his knee. "Let's find out. Let's go ahead with our original plans but with an eye out to the airship. We're going to do lots," he said with that boyish enthusiasm that made Amundsen like him so much.

On May 21, 1925, the N-24 and N-25 took off from Spitsbergen and headed for the North Pole, which was some six hundred miles away. To save weight they did not take along radio equipment. Each plane carried almost eight thousand pounds, including a pilot, navigator, and mechanic. Amundsen was in one plane as navigator, Ellsworth in the other.

They flew for about six hours, taking notes of the surfaces below. Now and then they would lose sight of each other in the thick cloud formations. But then either the N-24 or the N-25 would emerge out of a cloud bank and the tiny figures would wave at each other.

At one point, using his arms as semaphores, Amundsen signaled for a landing below on what appeared to be open water. Amundsen's plane, the N-25, went into a dive through a cloud and Dietrichsen, Ellsworth's pilot, circled carefully to avoid the possibility of an air collision.

When the N-24 emerged through a cloud, the N-25 was nowhere to be seen. They circled for a few minutes, but soon one of the motors gave a terrible bang and the propeller whirred slower and slower and came to a dead stop. There was nothing to do but try to make the open water below.

But the ice shifted rapidly and they came in too low, too late, and too fast. There was a tearing, ripping sound as they bounced on an ice floe and tore up the water to the next floe, from which they careened to a third, then a fourth, and finally a fifth. With a crash the Dornier buried its nose in a snow embankment and the propeller of the good motor was twisted out of all recognition.

Amundsen had fared somewhat better, though not much. As they were circling in preparation for a landing, the N-25 began to develop motor trouble. The engines coughed and sputtered and no amount of feathering would make them come quite alive. They prepared for a crash-landing, strapped themselves in securely, and Riiser-Larsen carefully, carefully let it lose altitude, let it out a bit more, stopped the motors completely—and they were practically floating into the bit of blue below when a sudden gust lifted the plane, as a swell lifts a boat, and catapulted them into a snowbank at least half a mile from their goal. The plane shuddered, rocked, and buried itself deeply in the embankment.

Almost a full day went by before the two parties found each other. Each plane was equipped with a small canvas boat and Ellsworth, rowing about the frosty lagoons, finally spotted Amundsen on a hill swiveling his glasses about the horizon in a search for the N-24. There was a shouting back and forth and Amundsen seized a megaphone ("That man thinks of everything," said Ellsworth) and blared, "All safe?" Ellsworth semaphored that they were.

Soon the six men were journeying back and forth inspecting both planes. They decided that the N-25 was in better shape and they then removed all the gasoline from the N-24 and by dint of great effort transported it in cans. Again the N-24 was inspected and "cannibalized" of parts that the N-25 would need.

Amundsen shot the sun and announced that they were about one hundred and forty miles from the North Pole. "Are you pleased?" he asked his partner.

"I'm delighted," Ellsworth responded with that boyish grin.

"Don't worry, we'll get out somehow. I always have," said Amundsen.

"I know that, sir," Ellsworth said with that air of hero worship he always used when talking with his chief.

That night they had a party in the cramped quarters of the N-25. They ate royally off a polar bear that Amundsen had shot, and drank some of Amundsen's favorite gin, then they tucked in "like sardines," one man's head at the other's feet.

They remained on the desolate spot almost a month. Ells-worth said he was glad they didn't have the radio with them. "Perhaps help would come," he said.

Omdal, who was his mechanic, grinned. "That would spoil your fun, wouldn't it? No fear, no one will come to save us."

Now and then, when game was scarce, Amundsen cut their rations in half. "We may have to winter here unless we can fix up the plane, get it out of the snow, build a runway, and take off." October, which was five months away, would mean the dark, endless night and the big freeze.

After several conferences they decided that they were lucky to be alive and in good health, with no one injured in the two crashes. The second decision was not so unanimous. Riiser-Larsen was doubtful they could build a runway to take the plane up. He was all for trying to make it on foot to Green-land.

Amundsen said that, if they were to try to get back to safety on foot, the latest possible date to start would be June 15. "That would give us a chance before winter closes in. But I vote we stay with the plane." It was his opinion that in a few weeks there would be sufficient thaw to enable them to drag the plane to open water.

They agreed to put off the actual decision until the middle of June and to let Amundsen, the leader, have the last word. Meantime the N-25 was lodged on an incline, the ice below having shifted. Amundsen ordered work done on a slide and, with great effort, the plane was finally nosed over with the help of the two motors, which were in good running order. But the ice below was very thin and the Dornier plowed a gamut of a thousand feet before it was brought to a halt.

That night there was a crackling, snapping sound. Amundsen awakened from his usual light sleep. "The ice is closing in," he shouted. He knew the ominous sound well.

All hands were routed out to empty the plane of all its contents, in order to lighten it. Then, at Amundsen's order, they began a rocking motion so that the ice would close in below rather than along the sides. "It'll be crushed like a tin can, otherwise," he said.

For the next three weeks they worked like savages trying to clear a runway. They were starved and begged for more food, but Amundsen kept a firm hand on the larder. A cup of nourishing chocolate for breakfast, and two biscuits—that was all for each man. He banned lunch completely and for dinner he permitted only a cup of soup made from the bones and shreds of the bear. No other game had been sighted. "We may not see any for months," he warned sternly.

Finally the runway was cleared. It was impossible to make it longer than about one-third of a mile. Theoretically the Dornier needed almost a mile of take-off elbow room before it could take to the air. But ahead of their crude runway there was a small lagoon ringed with ice. And turn the plane as they would in any other direction, there was nothing but huge hummocks of ice.

They made a trial run. The motors idled along to see if the surface would hold the plane. It did not—the surface was too soft with snow. The N-25 just plowed a deep furrow. There was but one thing to do and that was to clear the snow until they reached the bedrock of clear ice.

To do this they had to dig and cast aside innumerable tons of snow two feet deep and a third of a mile long. No sooner were they through than a heavy snow fell and they had to start all over again. The thin fare and the exhausting labor made them quarrelsome. But Amundsen maintained a firm hand. Riiser-Larsen was all for taking the chance of the four-hundred-mile trek on foot. Amundsen was adamant. Then Omdal suggested that they use the plane to clear away the snow. "Let's run it down to the edge of the lagoon. That will make the snow fly in all directions," he urged. But again the leader demurred. "We will surely run it into the water and then we'll be in trouble, for it'll freeze in fast some night."

So back they went to the back-breaking, snow-shoveling job. Though he was now fifty-three, Amundsen worked with them—never complaining. Soon he was receiving the same admiration bestowed on him by his former crewmen on the *Gjoa* and the *Maud*.

On June 15 all was in readiness. Now came the most anxious moment in Amundsen's life. They all stowed away in the crowded quarters in the cockpit. Everything but food had to be left behind. "We may crash and need the food," Amundsen said grimly. "If we get through, we're only about six hours from safety and steak. If we don't, we're five months away."

The motors sang in the frosty air. Riiser-Larsen, at the controls, cocked an ear and smiled with pleasure. "So far, so good," he murmured.

He held the brakes and stepped up the power. The plane lurched forward, straining for the air. He stepped more power into it, and it lurched and rocked like a small ship in a big storm. Still he held the brakes fiercely. There was a tremendous roaring of baffled power and, when he knew he could not hold the plane any more, the pilot let it go with a rush in order to gain impetus and make up for the short runway.

The N-25 almost leaped forward, bumped, ground against the slick ice, skidded round, righted, swirled again the other way and, like a loping dog running sideways, careened with breath-taking speed toward the lagoon and disaster but, instead, took sluggishly to the air and held there as Riiser-Larsen pulled the "stick" way back.

The motors whined and complained, but the N-25 gained altitude. Though the temperature was twenty degrees below zero, their faces were streaming with perspiration. They shook hands all around as the plane lifted into the clear sky.

"Let's have a look at our camp," Amundsen suggested.

Riiser-Larsen circled and below them were the things they had thrown out of the plane, with the bear's head atop everything. Ellsworth had wanted to take it home as a souvenir but reluctantly surrendered it on command.

After five hours a freeze set in and the pilot said he was having trouble with his stabilizers, which apparently were coated with ice—the usual hazard in those days. It was to be many years before de-icers were installed on aircraft. But he fought and fought and the congealing ice cracked and soon, through a dim haze, they could see land.

Their gasoline was getting very low; but they made it to Spitsbergen, landed in the angry, black water, ran smartly to a pier, got out and announced themselves.

The outpost could not believe it. "You are all believed dead," they heard on all sides. "No one writes my obituary without my permission," Amundsen growled. "I'll tell them when to write it."

Oslo put on a great fete for the returned heroes who brought back invaluable observations and data on air travel in the frozen North. Indeed, much of their material paved the way for the establishment of today's regular air services over the North Pole. Too, they sent data on their weather findings

to observatories throughout the world. This information was
of such primary importance that it started the development of
modern weather flights.

Amundsen wired Colonel Umberto Nobile of the Italian
air army to come to Oslo and discuss the possibility of selling
the airship N-1. Nobile arrived with a proposal from Mussolini. The Duce offered the N-1 as a gift if in return Amundsen
would agree to sail it over the North Pole under the Italian
flag. The world press had been criticizing the brutality of his
regime, and the fascist leader was anxious to establish Italy
as a civilized nation interested in scientific exploration.

The explorer was very short with the pompous, strutting
little man who wore his medals on his overcoat. "I am a citizen of Norway and any journey I make by land, sea, or air
will be under the flag of my country. What is your price."

The Italian bridled and tried to argue. But Amundsen was
now irritated. "Tell your master that my nationality and my
services are not for sale. What is your price?" he asked again.

There was a deal of quibbling before Nobile finally said his
government would wish seventy-five thousand dollars. He had
plans of the N-1 with him. After several conferences Amundsen said that, if the ship were overhauled so that it would have
a stiff nose instead of a soft one, he would buy. The N-1 was
a semidirigible. That is, it could not be moored to a hitching
post, though it was of the routine Zeppelin type made famous
during World War I.

The terms were agreed upon and they arranged to sign the
contract in Rome, where Mussolini could be present for the
purposes of publicity. Amundsen demurred but finally consented. He did not like the little dictator and all he stood for

and wanted to do. He was not impressed with strutting men. He had seen them collapse under the slightest hazard.

While the N-1 was being revamped, Ellsworth returned to the United States to attend to family matters. Amundsen decided to go along with him and try another lecture tour so that he might have some share in the purchase price. He did not wish to depend on Ellsworth completely, for he thought it was unfair to do so.

And so it was that Roald Amundsen, indefatigable and with the same fever that had possessed him in his youth, again began to plan an epoch-making flight that was to give him added luster. His face was lined and craggy from the rigors he had experienced, but his unquenchable love for the ice burned fiercely.

CHAPTER XIII

The Flight to the Top

On March 29, 1926, Mussolini, attired in cutaway and wing collar, formally handed over the N-1 to Amundsen representing the Kingdom of Norway. There had been some difficulty, before that ceremony, when Nobile demanded that the crew of the *Norge,* as it was christened, be composed only of Italians. To this ultimatum Amundsen gave his contemptuous refusal.

"We fly under the flag of Norway and the flag of the United States represented by my co-commander, Mr. Lincoln Ellsworth. Take it or leave it. If it's no, we go home."

The *Norge* sailed north for Kings Bay. There they found Commander Richard E. Byrd, the famous polar explorer and aviator. Byrd was planning to fly over the Pole and Amundsen wished him nothing but the best. He was not in a race with the plane, for one thing. For another, he admired Byrd, who had led many expeditions, and he realized that the *Norge* would have to drop all its plans and fly to the rescue if Byrd were forced down.

To everyone's relief the Byrd plane made the round trip in something like sixteen hours. There was a gay party that night on the *Chantier,* Byrd's ship, to which Amundsen and his crew were invited. The *Josephine Ford,* Byrd's plane, moored alongside, was bedecked with flowers and garlands. When Amundsen heard that all of Byrd's equipment had been given to him as a gift and that his crew were all volunteers, he said with feeling, "What an uplifted and splendid country you come from!" He knew whereof he spoke, though he loved his own country.

At last the day came for the *Norge* to take off. The plan called for an intercontinental flight, the first in history, across the North Pole from northern Europe to northern America, with the destination at Point Barrow, Alaska.

Rations for eighty days were taken aboard. Many of Amundsen's old friends were part of the crew. There was Riiser-Larsen, who was to be the second navigator—after Nobile. Then there was Dr. Finn Malmgren, the great meteorologist who was with Amundsen on the ill-fated *Maud;* Oscar Wisting, also of the *Maud;* Omdal, the mechanic, and for the first time a relative of Amundsen, his nephew Lieutenant Gustav Amundsen, who served as quartermaster.

The explorer was opposed to taking along a relative, because he had never done so. But he was persuaded by Riiser-Larsen, who was a good friend of the youth.

Gas was pumped in from containers brought from Europe; the *Norge* was checked for weight, and extraneous supplies were dumped out. All was set for the classic voyage.

The preceding year, Amundsen and Ellsworth had made arrangements to supply exclusive stories to *The New York Times* in return for the sum of fifty-five thousand dollars. This helped in part to defray the one-hundred-thousand-dollar investment Ellsworth made in the N-1.

During the course of these and other negotiations the two leaders came into constant conflict with Nobile. There was acrimony on both sides and, when the *Norge* was about to take off, Amundsen was not especially happy about the fact that Nobile was to be the chief navigator. Nobile also insisted that, as navigator, he would have the right to return to Italy with the ship if he deemed it best. Amundsen informed him that he was simply a "chauffeur" and had to take orders. Besides, the schedule flight was to take them over the Pole to Alaska.

However, all difficulties were forgotten when the lines were cast off, on May 11, and the great silver cigar rose in the air, turned slowly, and faced the north. It floated for a while, gathered speed, and made off into the gloom.

The noise of the motors was barely perceptible, the ship floated along with easy grace, and the crew felt as though they were suspended forever between heaven and earth. The sky seemed near and the earth below looked like a curious map— the sort of thing one sees in a child's geography book.

The gondola rocked and swayed, but they soon became accustomed to the motion. Nobile, ever nervous and short-tempered, went about checking on the men.

From on high, Amundsen and Ellsworth looked down at the deceptively smooth and treacherous land. "Looks as though any spot is a good spot to land a plane, doesn't it?" asked Ellsworth. "But it's not so when you get closer." They knew better than anyone else how ridges of snow and pinnacles of ice blend together to form the illusion of a smooth surface.

At the request of the great Curie Institute of Paris, Ellsworth devoted most of the trip to taking observations of the electricity in the atmosphere. He was supplied with a special instrument for the purpose. Amundsen, as leader, watched the weather, the navigation, the instruments, the crew, the food preparation, the watches for those who were to be on duty, the health and spirit of everyone.

The ease with which they were passing over his old friends, the snow, the ice, the turbulent waters, made him smile but he also felt a pang. He recalled the hard days of running with dog sleds; the encompassing, devouring frost; the gigantic, cascading waves. And he smiled wistfully and said, "This is a picnic—if nothing happens."

The course was set directly for the Pole. There they were to turn southerly and head for Point Barrow, Alaska, and then for Teller, on the Bering Sea. Amundsen's chief preoccupation was to watch out, from the lofty height, for a possible Arctic continent.

There were several near mishaps, all because of Nobile's nervousness and palpable lack of stability for his job as navigator.

Once, while speeding over the barren, icy wastes heading straight for the Pole, Nobile took over the control of the *Norge*. The wheelsman surrendered the wheel and the pompous man whirled it about to "see how she would handle."

Down went the *Norge* at great speed, with an iceberg looming up rapidly from below. Amundsen was about to spring forward and shake the man loose, for he seemed frozen with terror, when Riiser-Larsen seized the wheel and brought the nose of the dirigible up again. Amundsen ran to the back to determine whether the rear motor had been ripped loose, so close had the *Norge* come to the peak of the berg.

During another, similar emergency Riiser-Larsen actually

barked at Nobile, his superior, to right the wheel. The man was a famous designer of dirigibles, but he seemed no good at all in action.

Then came a time when they ran into an endless, thick fog. There was danger that a downward spiral of wind would send them crashing onto the ice or that they might hit an iceberg. Nobile pointed the nose upward but so suddenly and at such an angle that there was danger of the gas bags exploding under the atmospheric pressure of too high an altitude. Moreover, the perilous tilt terribly strained the delicate struts which held the whole dirigible together. He did not appear to know what was happening as crewmen lost their footing and went scrambling.

Suddenly he screamed, "Get to the bow. Get to the bow." Several of the crew ran to the bow to force the ship down by their weight.

When the *Norge* was approaching the Pole, Nobile, as navigator, should have known it in advance. But he made no mention of it until Amundsen, who had just taken a sight, said, "We will be over the Pole in one hour."

Beautifully enough, it was Ellsworth's birthday. "A birthday present for you, my boy," said Amundsen. "Thank you, sir," said Ellsworth, thrilled. Nor was Amundsen any less thrilled. With Ellsworth he stared down at the spot they were nearing. Then, with formality, both men at the same time threw down the Stars and Stripes and the Norwegian flag. They fluttered, whirled, and fell.

Just then Nobile came running with dozens of Italian flags, which he cast overboard. 'He'll frighten the seals," Amundsen said dryly. But the Italian was not yet through. He came running with a gigantic fascist flag, which he also threw overboard. It almost got caught in the motor propeller and, had it snagged, it might have meant the end of the *Norge*. "That man will be the death of me," said Amundsen, not knowing how truthfully he spoke.

He had now been to both Poles—the first man in history. He went to his bunk, lay down, and closed his eyes. But he didn't sleep. He was thinking of the boy he had been. With all his adolescent hopes and vanities, he had never thought— even in his wildest dreams—that he would accomplish all of this.

He felt tears coursing down his cheeks. "Is this emotion or is it senility?" he chided himself. But he knew it was emotion. He had done it! He had done more than he had hoped to do. The moment was a triumph—the climax of his whole life.

Meanwhile the ship was speeding along over the sea. No sight of land yet. Radio reports were coming in with great frequency from the powerful station at Svalbard, or Spitsbergen. Amundsen was also filing his articles with the stations, which were in turn flashing them to *The New York Times*.

Head winds came up and they bucked along. The motors were purring smoothly, but they were using more fuel than they had thought. Once again Nobile, who was supposed to know the consumption of the ship, for he had designed it, was at fault. But Amundsen refused to bicker with him and asked Riiser-Larsen how much farther they had to go. After a few minutes the assistant navigator said, "About two hundred and eighty miles, by my reckoning, to Teller."

The explorer asked how much fuel was left. "Seven hours' worth." Amundsen suggested mildly to Nobile that perhaps speed should be maintained at fifty miles an hour. "To allow for unforeseen contingencies in case we can't find a landing spot quickly," he said.

The lookout shouted, after six hours, "Land ho! Land ho!" Everyone rushed to see. It was land ahead. They had made the transcontinental flight over the Pole.

This was confirmed when a radio bearing came to them from Nome. They were definitely on the other side of the world and beating up on the northerly side of Kotzebue Sound.

There was nothing to do now but land. The strain on the crew had been tremendous but had gone unnoticed. Now the cheers and the hugging showed the emotion under which they were all laboring.

Around Cape Prince of Wales they went and bore in. There in the distance were the lights of a small town. The crew stood about shaking their heads with wonderment. They had floated in a motor-driven balloon a distance of thirty-two hundred miles in a matter of only about seventy-two hours.

Amundsen gave high praise to Riiser-Larsen as he was guiding the ship in for a landing in a bucking wind. According to the course the assistant navigator had set, they were only about ten miles off the beam when they sighted Point Barrow—an amazing feat for the time.

The airship majestically sailed into the tiny town. A child noticed the gigantic silver cigar in the early hours of the morning. Soon the whole population of Teller was gathered on the shore staring up at the fantastic spectacle.

Lower and lower the ship came. An anchor was thrown out and it scrabbled across the ice but failed to hold. Again the great ship luffed up and the anchor took hold and tugged the balloon back.

The gondola struck the ice and rebounded like a rubber

ball, for it was cushioned with a huge spring designed just for this purpose. Again the gondola bounced; the anchor held; ropes were thrown out and were seized by the townsfolk, who pulled mightily. This time the gondola settled and rested firmly. The anchor was made secure and out stepped the tired, unshaven men as though from another planet.

That evening the people of Teller gathered to hear about the amazing flight and to listen to these men from across the top of the world. The crew ate and drank as though they had never dined before. Amundsen was familiar with the emotional reaction. He recalled how, after he had negotiated the Northwest Passage, he sprang up the rigging and gulped chunks of raw caribou meat. They sang half the night and even dour Nobile joined in with several soft Italian airs.

It was now the job of the crew, led by Nobile, to dismantle the dirigible, pack it, and make it ready for shipping back to Europe in crates. Amundsen and Ellsworth pushed on to Nome to tell the world by telegraph of the successful flight and landing. But as soon as they had left, Nobile commanded the radio operator to flash the news that he had triumphed. Under his contract he was a paid employee and it was understood that all publicity about the flight would emanate from Amundsen and Ellsworth. When they got to Nome they shook their heads sadly, not at all astonished that Nobile had violated his pledge.

Roaring crowds, cavalcades of cars, and officials in silk hats were waiting to greet Amundsen and Ellsworth when they arrived in Seattle. With them was Nobile, who had joined them in Nome. The two leaders of the expedition, not expecting any fanfare, were wearing rough shirts and heavy coats. Nobile, by contrast, broke out in a gilded uniform of the

Italian army. When the *Victoria*, the ship they came in on, tied up, the little knot of distinguished officials almost missed the two plainly dressed men but fastened on Nobile, who accepted their attention blandly. The leaders could scarcely retain their laughter. It was funny to see him strut about shaking hands.

The trip home across the United States was a pageant of one reception after another. En route they were cheered at every station. A special car had been reserved for them by the Great Northern Railway and here they slept and ate in luxurious privacy. Telegrams arrived with every stop, and at every station a crowd was waiting to see Amundsen and Ellsworth.

At times the great train was held up while speeches were made and flowers presented to the bearded Norwegian who had no time even to shave. There were parties and banquets in St. Paul and at several stops en route to Chicago. Here they changed trains and, with relief, settled down to rest and talk and gaze at the landscape. But New York went wild. There to greet them, at the head of a great delegation of cars, stood their friend Commander Byrd.

Then came the usual ticker-tape parade. The police sirens led the way as they went up Broadway, out to Brooklyn, back to New York and up Fifth Avenue with perhaps a million people lining the curb and three thousand policemen out to hold them back.

At last they went aboard the *Bergensfjord* to sail for Europe. Their huge staterooms, which were made available free of charge, were decked with flowers, hampers of wine and whisky and fruits, and poems written by schoolchildren.

Amundsen unashamedly put his grizzled, balding head in

his arms and cried. "I am sorry, boy," he said to Ellsworth. "I am tired."

"No, sir, you are not tired," answered Ellsworth. "You will never be tired. Never in your life."

"I owe a great deal to you," said the explorer.

"You are mistaken, sir. Meeting you and sharing with you what you let me share have been the greatest experiences of my life. You allowed me to help you make history. I'm very grateful, sir."

The two men stood quietly smiling at each other and gripping hands.

They docked at Bergen, Norway, just about two months after the *Norge* had lifted its silvery body into the air for the flight. The whole city declared a holiday. The celebration was fantastic. People wept in the streets and hugged one another as the pair toured the city in an open limousine. "Our Roald!" they shouted. The houses were decked with banners and streamers hailing "Roald and the American, Ellsworth."

Here again Amundsen broke down, but no one noticed. It wasn't until later, when they were on board another steamer going to Oslo, that Amundsen confessed that he was very unhappy. "I have no place to go to now. I am old. I have nothing to do but sit like an old man and write my memoirs. I am finished."

Ellsworth laughed. "You will never be finished. I promise you will die on the ice."

"Do you think so?" Amundsen asked eagerly.

Then they both roared.

Oslo put on a parade of floats, each depicting the great incidents in Amundsen's life. There was the tiny *Gjoa,* the broad-beamed *Maud,* the two Dorniers, the *Norge* . . . and following all of them was a life-size replica of Amundsen on a sledge behind a team of Huskies.

"They made a mistake," Amundsen whispered. "I always ran in front of the beasts."

The two leaders were formally received by the King and thanked. Not long thereafter they parted, Ellsworth to return to America. They were to see each other only once more, when Amundsen went to the United States on a lecture tour. The ever-youthful Ellsworth, who died in 1951, had a vast section of Antarctica named after him when he flew over the uncharted region in 1935. He never forgot the rugged Norseman whom he considered the greatest explorer of the century.

CHAPTER XIV

Viking's Last Voyage

Amundsen went to his modest house outside of Oslo. It was one of the things he was able to buy back since his bankruptcy. Here he sat and dreamed, answered letters from learned societies and old friends, refused invitations, and looked longingly at the sea. He tired more often than was his wont, but he ascribed this lassitude to his inactivity.

Now and then he went to Oslo to see old friends. Wherever he went, people pointed and said, "Look, there's our Roald." Without doubt—in Norway, at any rate, and in the world press—he was the foremost living explorer.

His greatest pleasure was to go to the museum and gaze through the glass cases at the exhibits he had brought back from the ends of the earth. There were the soft Eskimo moccasins, the exquisite caribou-fur blankets, the dainty undergarments for children, the long needles. The attendants knew him and nodded respectfully.

He soon realized that this life was not for him. The respectful nods especially irritated him. "I'm not a has-been yet," he shouted. But the world persisted in treating him as such.

"I've outlived my usefulness to myself. I'm just a living

monument," he said fiercely when newspapermen came to see him. He felt especially bad when young would-be explorers begged for a visit. While he was kind and helpful to them, as others had been to him, he rebelled against the idea of retirement and the horizontal life.

He went over the list of other explorers of his day and found that he had accomplished more than they. Admiral Peary, for example. He had just been to the North Pole and had stopped after that. Scott made the South Pole and died. Nansen discovered a drift method. All had become famous household names. He had done much more, Amundsen told himself angrily; he, too, was a household name. But he was dissatisfied. There must be something he could do.

He decided to travel a bit. In comfort. He went to America and arranged for a lecture tour. He found to his amazement that Nobile had been going up and down the land telling of the adventures of the *Norge* and claiming all credit. The lecture bureaus which handled arrangements told Amundsen that they doubted whether his tour would be successful in the wake of Nobile's.

He and Ellsworth sat up late one night talking endlessly about the impudence of the man. Amundsen's own tour was well received despite the gloomy predictions of the agents. With subtle sarcasm he never failed in any of his addresses to flail the "braggart," as he called Nobile. While he was furious, he held his anger in check in order the better to demolish, by word of mouth, the "pretender"—another epithet with which he labeled his former companion. The press agreed with him and the public agreed with him.

But in Italy it was another matter. Here the controlled fascist press, which printed only what it felt would please Mus-

solini, continued to hail Nobile. He was promoted from
Colonel to Commander and he "sold" the government on an
expedition of his own.

For this he was given funds by several Italian societies and
his native city of Milan and he proceeded to refit the *Norge*,
which was renamed the *Italia*. He also cabled attractive offers
to such stalwarts as Riiser-Larsen and asked them whether they
would come along at good salaries.

Riiser-Larsen cabled Amundsen, who smiled. "Why not?"
he answered by cable. "You may save his life."

According to the ambitious plans which he announced,
Nobile was going to explore the entire uncharted areas of the
Arctic in both hemispheres. He was going to do this, he said,
in a series of flights above the North American continent and
the Asiatic continent. All uncharted lands he found would be
named in honor of the Italian fascist state.

The most ambitious part of the program was to settle the
Italia at the North Pole itself, where he would stay for several
months studying weather in the name of fascist science.

The Duce placed a large vessel at his disposal. This would
serve as a main base and was to be stationed at Spitsbergen
with a crew complement of some one hundred and seventy
men. No expense was spared in loading her with food, gear,
radio equipment, and Arctic clothing.

A powerful radio station in Rome tuned itself to the *City of
Milan*, the luxurious base vessel, for constant, uninterrupted
communication. Mussolini himself was to be kept informed
daily as to the progress of the *Italia*.

On April 15, 1928, the *Italia* lifted into the sky after Commander Nobile was kissed on both cheeks by the Duce, who
was present at the ceremony. Bands played, flags waved, and

Nobile went forth for an exploration—with perhaps the most elaborate arrangements in history.

In May, Nobile tested the *Italia*. Its motors had undergone extensive alterations; better quarters had been provided for the crew; the most expensive and modern equipment had been installed.

After several trips over the Arctic Ocean, the *Italia* finally made its way over the Pole. (At the last minute Riiser-Larsen had refused to accompany a commander in whom he had no confidence.) The *Italia* radioed the glad news to the base ship, which in turn told Mussolini about it. There was festivity in Rome and Milan and aboard the *Italia*. A hamper of champagne, especially put aside for the occasion, was broken out and Nobile drank to the health of the dictator. The dictator, in turn, told the world in a special message that his government was devoted to science and exploration. He cited the flight of the *Italia* over the Pole.

The airship was making its way back to Kings Bay when it ran into a storm. Nobile radioed that the ship might turn for the west or the east. As yet, he was undecided. Meantime the *Italia* would keep in touch. It did. It ran into heavy fog and floundered, not knowing which way to turn. Ice began to form and the wheelsman reported that the *Italia* was not responding the way it should. Moreover, it was losing elevation.

Nobile at once ordered all ballast thrown overboard. In a fright he also ordered the gas valves opened lest the ship go too high and the atmospheric pressure burst the bags wide open.

Suddenly the *Italia* plunged at sickening speed to the ice; the gondola broke open, spilling men and equipment. Then it bounded up again and sailed away at furious speed with the six crewmen who had not been spilled. A long time later the debris of the *Italia* was discovered. None of the bodies was found. The ship, with its crew, had burned on the ice.

But Nobile and nine other men—six of them badly hurt—were dumped on the ice some three hundred miles from base. Nobile had a broken arm; they had some food—luckily some cases had been dumped out with them—and parts of the radio and little hope. The radioman, who was severely hurt, managed to patch together some of the sections and send a feeble SOS. This was heard by some ships at sea which could not trace the origin. They, in turn, notified Spitsbergen and the *City of Milan.*

The base was alarmed, for no signals had been heard for several hours. Nobile had been sending messages at a furious rate ever since the *Italia* had taken off, and especially since the successful flight over the Pole.

All civilized nations on the fringe of the Arctic put relief measures into motion. The Swedish air force sent out several planes, which circled a wide area. The Italian government began to organize a vast rescue operation. In Norway, Amundsen was hastily summoned to head a special committee which would determine the best means. When communication with the *Italia* was lost, it was May 25. Nothing was heard again until June 5, when a farmer living on the fringe of the pack said he heard a faint SOS on his radio.

By June 9 the survivors of the tragedy were in constant communication with their base. The news electrified the world. There was some hope that they might be reached. The signals were weak but stronger than they had been. No details were given except that several men were hurt and that the *Italia* itself was lost. No one was able to determine how this disaster could happen. But if the survivors could be reached in time, the story would be told. The radio signals complained about lack of food.

Several nations were now engaged in rescue operations that had become almost a contest to see which could find the survivors.

Because of his world-wide prestige, Amundsen was able to borrow a seaplane from France. Norway had none at all. A big Latham, complete with two competent pilots, was flown up from France. It landed at Tromsö, where Amundsen, ready with supplies to be dropped to the survivors, got aboard. He was accompanied by his old colleague Dietrichsen. The big plane took off, circled, and made for Spitsbergen. Amundsen planned to go to Kings Bay and use it as a base for a wide-circling series of flights.

Meantime ice breakers, seaplanes, and monoplanes by the score were flying over a great area. At last, one pilot spotted the survivors. Several of them had left the main body and decided to go on foot to find help. Their theory was that they could guide any searchers back to the spot where the injured were. But they were never heard from again.

With Nobile were three badly hurt men. He was taken off first and flown to the base. Then the plane went back to pick up the others, but crashed. It was not until two weeks later that an icebreaker rescued the survivors.

Meantime there was concern for Amundsen and his party. In the excitement over the rescue expedition for the *Italia* survivors, everyone had forgotten about the would-be rescuers. But few were troubled, because Amundsen was a skilled and seasoned man on the ice. "If anyone can take care of himself and his men, he can," was the consensus of opinion.

In Oslo, however, those who knew about Amundsen's dislike for Nobile shook their heads. "Imagine his coming out of retirement to hunt for the enemy he despises. And what if he should lose his own life in the attempt? That would be tragic." It *was* tragic. This sentiment was echoed in the press of the world after one of the Latham's pontoons was found floating off the Fugloe Islands just a few air minutes from Tromsö. Apparently the plane had developed engine trouble soon after taking off and had plunged into the sea.

And thus it was that Roald Amundsen died in the savage, beloved element he best understood. It is certain that he did not mind his sacrifice on behalf of a colleague whom he did not highly regard. For, as an adventurer in the icy jungles, he understood—better than most men—that disfavor does not go into the reckoning when a life is endangered. Toward Nobile, who lived to meet with not-unfounded sinister charges against himself, Amundsen would have reacted with his usual compassion and complete understanding.

Nobile spent a good many years of his life trying to disprove the charge not only that he was guilty of cannibalism but that he lacked personal courage in allowing himself to be air-lifted off the ice before his comrades. Amundsen, the strong and good man who stood by Dr. Cook, would not have raised a word of criticism against Nobile. For he comprehended utterly, as few men can, the strength and weakness of men in peril of their lives.

Today, on the maps of the world, there is an Amundsen Gulf south of the Beaufort Sea in the Arctic region. And there is an Amundsen Sea northwest of the Walgreen Coast in the Antarctic. There is also a glacier named in honor of Amundsen, and it will be several millions of years before the pedestal and the geographic designation vanish from the earth. These are his monuments. No man can ask for more endurable trophies.

Bibliography

FIRST CROSSING OF THE POLAR SEA, by Roald Amundsen and Lincoln Ellsworth with chapters by other members of the Expedition; New York, George H. Doran Company, 1927

AMUNDSEN, THE SPLENDID NORSEMAN, by Bellamy Partridge; New York, Frederick A. Stokes Company, 1929

MY LIFE AS AN EXPLORER, by Roald Amundsen; Garden City, N. Y., Doubleday, Page & Company, 1927

VAGRANT VIKING, by Peter Freuchen; New York, Julian Messner, Inc., 1953

POLAR EXPLORATION, by Andrew Croft; London, A. C. Black, 1939

BEYOND HORIZONS, by Lincoln Ellsworth; Garden City, N. Y., Doubleday, Doran and Company, 1938

HEROES OF THE FARTHEST NORTH AND FARTHEST SOUTH, by John K. MacLean; New York, T. Y. Crowell Company, 1913

THE FIRST CROSSING OF GREENLAND, by Fridtjof Nansen; London, Longmans, Green & Company, 1906

THE COLD LANDS, by James Maurice Scott; London, Methuen & Company, 1939

CLOSE CALLS IN MY LIFE AS AN EXPLORER, by Roald Amundsen; New York, World's Work, June, 1927

The New York Times From 1895 Through 1929 With Special Attention to Dispatches Filed by Amundsen as Explorer-Correspondent

Index

Amundsen, Roald, Birth, 12; schooling, 12-17; hardens self to rigors of exploration, 14-16; mother, 13-17; military draft, 17-18; essays first dangerous journey, 18-28; steeps self in navigational studies, 29-30; signs for Antarctic Expedition and has first icebound experience, 31-34; assumes "first responsibility", 37; helps to free *Belgica*, 46-47; receives ship master's license, 51; studies at observatories, 52-53; purchases *Gjoa*, sails away under cloud of debt, 54-56; undergoes harsh tests as master, 61-62; immerses self in study of Eskimo culture, 72-86; unknowingly passes over North Magnetic Pole, 84-85; negotiates Northwest Passage, 88-91; lectures in U. S. and Europe on adventures, 100; buys the *Fram*, 103; plans "drift" theory, 103-105; learns about Peary's discovery, heads for South Pole, 106; sets up base, 108; plans South Pole dash, 104-117; South Pole victory, 127-128; world lauds him, 130-132; plans air expedition, 133-134; returns honors to Germany, 135; enters lucrative ship-building business, 136; designs *Maud*, 137-138; sails Northeast Passage, 139; injured, health impaired, 143; blasts out of ice, 144-145; restudies Eskimo culture, 147-148; Norwegian Gov't. votes him gift for exploration, 148-149; studies polar exploration by air, 149-152; financially ruined, 152-154; meets Lincoln Ellsworth, new vistas open, 154-156; navigates N-25 and crashes, 158; flies in *Norge* over North Pole, 166-175; goes into retirement, 177; engages in rescue operations for Nobile, 182; the "Viking" is lost in rescue effort, 183; names on maps of the world, 183-184

Antarctica, Amundsen's first visit, 32-49; plans and makes South Pole dash, 102-130

Arctic, Voyages in *Gjoa*, 54-91; voyages in *Fram*, 103-105; sails Northeast Passage, in *Maud*, 137-138; flies in *Norge* over North Pole

Baffin Bay, 61
Balboa, Vasco Nunez de, 13
Banks Island, 59